SELF-DEVELOPMENT AND TRANSCENDENCE

SELF-DEVELOPMENT AND TRANSCENDENCE

EFFECTIVE CONSCIOUSNESS AS THE GOAL OF PSYCHOTHERAPY

D. B. Clark

Writers Club Press

San Jose New York Lincoln Shanghai

Self-Development and Transcendence
Effective Consciousness as the Goal of Psychotherapy

Writers Club Press
an imprint of iUniverse.com, Inc.

For information address:
iUniverse.com, Inc.
5220 S 16th, Ste. 200
Lincoln, NE 68512
www.iuniverse.com

ISBN: 0-595-16068-9

Printed in the United States of America

In profound respect for all those counselees who gave me the ultimate respect of their trust, so that I might assist them as they challenged and changed their ineffective behaviors.

Introduction

Throughout the ages, philosophers and psychologists have struggled to create theories to explain human behavior. Those faced with the everyday problem of helping others to behave more effectively have used these theories to guide them in their work. As a Clinical Psychologist, I have also used these theories, but frankly I have never been satisfied with the guidance they gave me. While most of these theories explained some of the behavior I observed, no one theory explained most of the behavior. It seemed to me that some of the theories, which did attempt to be comprehensive, had become so distant from their basic assumptions that the relationship between their premises and working conclusions was difficult to follow and frequently obfuscated by esoteric terminology. And, of course, many of these theories contradict one another.

When confronted with this conflicting theoretical offering, it is fashionable to say that one is eclectic. Applying whatever seems applicable from a variety of theories is often the best one can do. But the use of eclecticism, especially when effective, may reinforce the feeling that human behavior is bewilderingly complex.

Perhaps it is my own unrealistic desire for greater security, but I have always wanted a way to understanding my counselees' behavior that was the opposite of complex, and almost always applicable. My longed for theory need not have given me instant understanding, but at least I wanted it to give me faith that I was beginning my search for understanding on the right pathway.

Maybe such theories already exist. Maybe I'm unable to accept these very adequate theories because my basic assumptions about human behavior are also too idiosyncratic. Maybe I'm just not patient or intelligent enough to follow the more complex theories. Be that as it may, in lacking faith in any of the existing theories, intellectual honesty and professional integrity made it necessary for me to create my own theory to guide me in my helping role.

In contemplating such a challenge, I realized how presumptuous I was. The issues I knew I must examine and resolve if I was to create a useful theory of human behavior are the core issues that have always confronted and confounded our greatest thinkers—consciousness, freewill, the mind-body problem, and the nature of the self. Did I really expect to succeed where others have so often despaired?

The answer is, I had to try. Then, though I might not have resolved these profound issues to anyone else's satisfaction, I would have at least reached my own conclusions. Even if my theory does not turn out to be an accurate reflection of reality, I should still be a more effective clinician than I was in the past. My arduous thinking will have given me greater assurance, however deluded, that I know what I am doing, and I will be freer from doubt and better able to focus on my counselees' concerns rather than on my own.

Contents

Preamble

Self-Development: *the progression in organizational complexity of the human central nervous system that a human being may proceed through in the process of maturing.*

Given a normal human central nervous system and a supportive social environment, a human being will inevitably develop through six levels of self-integration, the Affective or Limbic-Self, the Content or Cerebral-Self, the Invested-Self, Consciousness or the Functional-Self, the Self-Aware-Self, and the Self-Concept-Self.

The development of the next two levels, the Integrated-Self and the Transcendent-Self are not inevitable. In fact, their development may be exceptions in human development rather than the rule.

Self-Transcendence is of two types:
1. functioning at a level of effective consciousness.
2. functioning as a self that is so identified with that which is greater than self that one is more than the individual self,

Self-development and self-transcendence will be fully defined and explained in the theoretical section of this book, and effective consciousness will be defined and explained in the application section.

The Theory

First There is Life

Wondering Why

We continue to ask the "why" questions. Why did we come into being? Why or for what purpose do we continue to exist? As science and technology advance, more and more of the "how" questions are answered, and our lives are more convenient, secure, diverse, and exciting. It would seem that we would be satisfied with so many practical answers to so many practical questions. But our conveniences just allow us more time to ask why.

Why do we want to know why? Presumably because we believe that an answer to this question would make us feel better. At least we would feel more assured, in the face of inevitable adversity, that there is some reason to tolerate life's unpleasant feelings. Therefore, through the ages we have given ourselves more or less reassuring answers to the two eternal questions: "What is the first cause of life and what is its ultimate purpose?" For example, God caused life to come into existence. Furthermore, God intends that we should follow His laws so that we may be worthy of eternal life after death—and also to avoid eternal damnation.

Others, not inclined toward theological explanations have found reassurance in the belief that science will eventually know how and, therefore, perhaps even why life began. Knowing our causes and having faith in our technology, we may also assume that science will eventually

1

give us the power to control and select our own destiny—which might or might not be eternal life but certainly will not be eternal damnation. We are reassured by these answers to our "why" questions—as long as we do not examine our answers too closely, as long as we do not ask why God came into being, or as long as we do not remind ourselves that the ultimate cause in scientific theory might be chance.

But even if our reasoning was more precise there would be a problem with using scientific reasoning to reassure ourselves. Reasoning is a process. If a process is to be a process, it must be *in* process. It must be active, on-going, unresting. In other words, it must be alert to new information that would call into question whatever reassuring explanations we had previously created. Therefore, reasoning creates new uncertainties, new unpleasant feelings. We are seeking the feeling of assurance that comes from final answers, and reasoning seems to lead only to perpetual questions. It would be nice to have reasoned answers, but it would be even nicer to have firm beliefs.

There might be those who are satisfied with faith alone. Such people are enviable. But this book is addressed to those who may have been cursed by too much reasoning, who might have lost some of the capacity for faith, who might be able to gain assurance only if faith is supported by a reasoned structure.

This book is intended to provide a reasoned structure for those who need such structure. This book is concerned with self-development and transcendence, with why the self came into being and why the self continues to exist. In other words, this book is concerned with the aspect of life that is probably most important to us—our own selves.

Minimal Criteria for a Reassuring Theory

How must the reasoned explanations set forth in this book be structured so as to provide the maximum amount of assurance for those inclined toward doubting? What minimal criteria must a theory of self-development meet for the reasoning person to have the highest probability of feeling assured?

Criteria for an Acceptable Theory My own reasoning suggests that the following criteria must be met if you are to be assured by this theory of self-development and self-transcendence:

1. A theory of self must relate to what we already know about our own selves; it must have commonsense validity.
2. The theory must have internal consistency. There must be no logical contradictions between the assumed premises of the theory and the conclusions drawn from those premises.
3. The theory must not contradict too many of the other generally held theories or verified facts about self-development.
4. The theory must provide, if not prediction, at least guidance for our future behavior.

If I can describe a theory of self-development and transcendence that meets these criteria, will you feel a greater degree of assurance, of comfort in knowing why you have developed as you have developed?

Perhaps. I hope so. But if I can clearly articulate such a theory, at least *I* will be assured. After all, if I am motivated to do this much reasoning then I must be one of those who is most in need of assurance.

Reasoning by Analogy About the Formal Organization of Life

We need to eventually arrive at a common-sense definition of "self." But, for the time being, let us assume that the self with which we are most concerned is the living self. Therefore, to begin our understanding of the self we must make assumptions about the nature of life. What distinguishes life from non-life, or organic matter from inorganic matter? In raising such questions, we always raise even more basic questions.

What is matter? What distinguishes matter from non-matter? In the Bible, we may trace our ancestry back to Adam and Eve and then assume that God created Adam and Eve. But who created God? Likewise, we may trace organic matter back to inorganic matter, and inorganic matter back to "the big bang." But what existed before the big bang? Just as with "why" questions, "how" and "what" questions lend themselves to infinite regression. We can always ask ourselves why or what caused "the first cause" to happen, and backward forever. However, if we are to go forward rather than infinitely backwards, we must begin somewhere. We must make an assumption about the point in the past when the past began to effect the future. Insofar as self-development is concerned, I am making the assumption that the initial point in the evolution of the self is that point at which life is differentiated from non-life. I am not assuming that, because life occurred, the development of the self was inevitable. Rather, I am assuming the self could never have occurred unless at some time in the distant past life initially occurred.

This then is my first appeal to commonsense. If you are "comfortable" with this assumption then it may be worth your while to continue reading.

My second assumption is that life and non-life are made of the same matter. The atoms that make up that which is living do not differ in their nature from the atoms that make up that which is non-living. What does differ between living and non-living matter is the organization of the atoms within these two kinds of matter. We have established the convention that living matter always contains the element carbon. We have settled on this convention because we have yet to find that which we call life in the absence of carbon. But the presence of carbon does not guarantee life. It is the organization of the various particles of matter, including carbon, that defines the presence of life. **"Life"** *is a particular organization of otherwise non-living matter that has as its defining characteristic the potential for maintaining its organization and the tendency to do so.*

The third defining characteristic and assumption about living matter is that it is unstable. A molecule of water is stable. The electrical bonding between its atoms of oxygen and hydrogen resist change and, therefore, water remains water until great force is applied to break the molecular bond. The organization of those carbon-based molecules that we define as life tends to be far more complex than that of simple molecules such as water and, moreover, relatively little force is required to disrupt the organization of living matter. The capacity of living matter to resist the disruption of its organization is not found in the electrical bonding within molecules but rather in the manner in which these bonds are organized. By definition then, **living matter** *is matter in which the organization of its components is such that it is able to resist the disruption of its organization.*

Why did this life, this particular organization, come into existence? Did God decree that it should be, or was it chance? You will have to make our own assumptions about this step backward into infinite regression. I am merely assuming that once this peculiar organization, which is life, came into being, the organization, by definition, tended to perpetuate its organization and to resist those forces that would disrupt its organization. Once life, as defined, is begun then its all-consuming concern becomes how to perpetuate its organization. So **life** *is an unstable organization of otherwise non-living matter.*

What is the nature of this organization that enables it to perpetuate its organization? What follows are more assumptions, assumptions about how life works, assumptions that are based primarily on analogous reasoning, since "facts" are hard do come by at this level of conceptualization and tend often to be based on what is known to work on an observable level.

Life's Progressive Organizational Integration

Since life is an unstable organization, and an unstable organization that exists in a less organized, ever-changing environment, there are constant forces that could cause life to change its organization. One factor governing the stability of an organization is the complexity of the organization. It might be assumed that the simpler the organization, the more stable the organization. But life is not found to be made up of simple molecules. What seems to give this complex living organization its increasing probability of stability is the nature of the integration of the molecular particles that make up living matter. By "**integration**" of **the parts within an organization**, I am referring to *the contact that each of the parts has with each of the other parts within the organization*. In general, the more integrated the parts of an organization the greater the stability. By analogy, using two nails, three boards could be nailed together in a straight line. Pressure placed on one end of this assembly might cause the three boards to collapse like a folding ruler. This would be a relatively unstable organization. If, on the other hand, the three boards were nailed end to end, as in a triangle, pressure on one end would result in less disruption of the structure. Greater contact between the various parts in an organization accounts for the greater stability of the organization.

It is assumed that, under the relentless pressure of the ever-changing environment to which initial life forms were subjected, it was more likely that those life forms that had the greatest integration of their various parts had the highest probability of maintaining their organizations. Therefore, it is assumed that one of the ways living organizations maintain their organizations is through becoming increasingly integrated.

But merely increasing the number of contacts among the parts of an organization is not enough to insure the maintenance of an organization. An effective arrangement of parts is an arrangement must probably be one that, to some degree, enables the individual parts to at times function as a whole to accomplish more than the individual parts can accomplish separately.

Integration is a matter of degree. Further reasoning by analogy, a low order of integration might be three rods lying in contact side by side. Pushing one outside rod on its side may disturb the other two rods and, therefore, the unit of rods might be said to operate as a whole. Pulling the outside rod, however, will leave the other two rods undisturbed. On the other hand, if the three rods are attached, end-to-end in a straight line, movement of any one of the rods will move the other two. Based on this analogy, it may be assumed that the integration of an organization is more effective when there is an increase in number of attachments of parts.

But too many points of attachment between the parts of an organization will result in an inability to more. Attach the three rods, with several nails at a joint, end to end in a triangle, and the individual rods now become immobile, and the triangle is vary stable but inflexible. Its stability is strength against a strong force, but weakness if flexibility is required and the individual rods should move aside in the face of an even stronger force. Therefore, it is assumed that **the most effective integration of an organization** *is one in which there is a maximum number of contacts between the various parts within an organization while still allowing differentiation of the various parts.* In other words, the optimally integrated organization is one in which the necessary functioning of one part is not impeded by its functional connection with other parts in the organization.

These simple assumptions about the formal nature of the effective integration of an organization seem to be descriptive of what has actually occurred in the evolution of the organization of human life. The enormously complex organization that is the human central nervous system is integrated beyond our current understanding and yet the individual parts also perform their unique functions. The integration is such that complex cooperation is possible but cooperation may also be suspended to allow differential functioning of parts.

To summarize, the eventual evolution of the self is made possible by the nature of living matter. **Life** *is a relatively unstable organization of non-living matter that tends toward increasing integration of its organization as a strategy for resisting disorganization.*

Finally, in defining life as an organization of matter that is motivated to maintain its organization, an interesting fact about life emerges—life seems to be an anomaly in the universe. All other organizations of matter seem to operate by the law of entropy. In other words, over time, there is a tendency for non-living matter to become less and less organized. Life resists entropy, and one of its strategies for resisting entropy is an increase in the complexity and integration of its organization.

The next chapter involves considerable speculation regarding the neurological level of this complexity and integration. Bear with me. I believe that this theoretical speculation must be understood and at least tentatively accepted if later speculation regarding the higher levels of self-development and functioning can be understood and accepted.

And the Self Evolves

The Integration of the Central Nervous System

It would be convenient if the relationship between the various parts of the central nervous system was simple and straightforward, and we could therefore wire and rewire the brain like we were Dr. Frankenstein refining his monster. Such simplistic theories of brain functioning are based upon hydraulic or electronic analogies. But following such simple and erroneous models of brain functioning has led neurophysiologists to despair of ever understanding such human capacities as speech and consciousness. Such analogies underestimate the enormous complexity and potential of organic matter. Integration and interaction in organic matter begins at the molecular level, as neurons interact within and between biochemicals. Interaction and integration proceeds as a possible ten thousand synaptic junctures are established between the dendrites of one neuron and the axons and cell bodies of other neurons. Integration proceeds as assemblages of such interacting neurons interact with other assemblages of interacting neurons. Clusters of these assemblages in one part of the neocortex interact with other neurons, neuron assemblages, and clusters of neuron assemblages in subcortical areas of the brain. With so many combinations and permutations possible, what could be impossible?

It must be acknowledged, however, that so many possibilities make understanding the nature and significance of all these possible interactions rather difficult. That is why it was essential that someone, such as Gerd Sommerhoff, (1974) with knowledge and talent in both the disciplines of Neurophysiology and Philosophy should create the necessary neurophysiological models to organize what would otherwise be chaos. Then, building upon Sommerhoff's detail analysis of neurophysiological functioning, a more global psychological model of the self may be constructed on a firmer foundation.

Gerd Sommerhoff's Logic of the Living Brain

"I touch my finger to the hot iron, and almost instantly I withdraw my finger." A simple mechanical model of heat expanding metal and triggering a spring to withdraw the finger might explain this phenomenon. Although this simple mechanical explanation might have been faulty, the fact that we could propose such a logically consistent explanation for a human reflex was at least a start. We did not yet know how human beings functioned but at least it seemed possible that an explanation was possible.

On the other hand, our explanations for other kinds of human behavior were not so reassuring. "The next day I see the iron, and as I am reaching toward it, I remember that it might burn me, so I withdraw my hand." This day, there was no heat to expand metal and trigger a spring release. What model or theory can I use to explain this new behavior? What do I mean when I say, "I *see* the iron."? I know that I would not have seen the iron had my eyes been closed. So I must have used my eyes to see the iron. But how did my eyes stop my hand from moving toward the iron? Yesterday, I burned my hand. But that was yesterday. How did I store the information of yesterday so that it would effect my behavior today? Even if I knew how and where I stored the information about yesterday's burn, how did that information stop my hand from moving toward the iron? What is more, who or what is this "I" that seems to be aware that I was burned by the iron and might again be burned by the iron if I reach forth my hand?

Long ago we learned that if we are hit on the head, at least temporarily we cease to be concerned with such questions. We also learned that if some people are damaged by blows to the head, thereafter they behaved in ways that suggested that they were no longer able to retain and process information about yesterday. Therefore, we came to suspect that the gray and white matter inside the head must have something to do with learning, memory, and the capacity to be aware.

But how does it work? The ancients proposed the explanation of an "homunculus"—a little man inside the brain pulling the levers to make the person perform. But was there another homunculus inside the brain of the first homunculus, and where would this infinite regression eventually end? Through the centuries, this mind-body or brain-body question has puzzled and frustrated thinkers. Although it was generally assumed that the brain is involved in such mental functions, we were unable to describe *mental* processes in those concrete, observable, verifiable ways that are necessary to give assurance to most scientifically trained thinkers. This continued frustration even led some neurophysiologists to conclude that the mind-brain-body problem is beyond the reach of the scientific method. They re-proposed the ancient solution that physical phenomena may be explained by physical laws but mental phenomena can only be explained by the assumption of another set of, as yet unknown, *mental* laws. Of course, since these mental laws are unknown, they must be taken on faith, and most of us, scientists or otherwise, are rather uncomfortable in depending upon *other* people's faith.

The majority of neurophysiologists, however, still put their faith in the scientific method. They assume, if they continue the struggle to understand the details of the anatomical structure and biochemistry of the brain, eventually all of these pieces will fall into place, and we will have a physically verifiable explanation for mental functioning that does not require a whole new universe of mental laws.

In the meantime, until this coalescing of details occurs, it is convenient and reassuring that Gerd Sommerhoff has been able to suggest how this mind-brain-body machine *might* logically be constructed. Sommerhoff believes that neurophysiologists might be more efficient in their search for the neurological connectors between physical and mental events if they are guided by a plan that is based upon what is generally known about brain matter, but logically extrapolated beyond the known. He proposed just such a plan in his book, *The Logic of the Living Brain* (Sommerhoff, 1974).

What is the location (or locations), and what is the nature of the neurological structure that contains this information: "If I touch the hot iron, I will be burned."? No neurophysiologist can as yet answer this question with certainty. Moreover, the variability across individual human brains, the complexity of the storage mechanism, and the sophisticated technology required to measure brain matter might mean that, for all practical purposes, the actual location of the information in a *specific* human brain will never be discovered. Sommerhoff, however, wished to demonstrate that the existence of such a neurological structure is *theoretically* possible. The articulation of this theoretical possibility may then guide the development of the research and technology that could eventually refine our knowledge of the general neurophysiological structures.

Mental Functions

For Sommerhoff, *the primary function of the central nervous system is the coordination of movement to enable the organism to reach goals.* Following Sommerhoff's reasoning, if my goal is to pick up the iron without burning myself, I must have within my central nervous system an "internal model of the external world." It would be impractical, however, and it would create another infinite regression problem, to assume that my internal model of the world would be an exact replica of all that is in the external world. The number of objects and actions relative to those objects in the external world, or universe, is infinite. Even the astronomically large number of combinations and permutations of synapses in my brain could not contain the infinite. Moreover, who or what in my brain is selecting from all of those infinite possibilities in the internal model just the right combinations of movements to allow me to pick up the iron without burning myself? Sommerhoff asserts "…that the "models" of the outside world that are formed in the brain consist of aggregates of expectations of how the subjective sensory inputs transform in consequence to the aggregates of self-induced movements open to us." The internal model and the neuron synaptic assemblage supporting that model would only be concerned with coordinating the sensory input of the iron to effect the motor output so as to move my hand in the proper direction. In my simplistic example, my "aggregate of expectancies" might concern only the handle of the iron. My aggregate of expectancy regarding the handle of the iron is: "If I touch the handle, I will either get burned or I will not get burned." My aggregate of self-induced movements includes touching the handle and not touching the handle. I exercise the movements of touching the handle, and I do not get burned. Then, my internal model of the external world contains the expectancy that the sensory input from my hand would be a sensation of coolness coming from the handle of the iron. I now experience this coolness. So, as far as survival is concerned, I may leave my hand on the handle. In this simple example of a sequencing of one choice following another, my internal models of the external world have succeeded in guiding my movements and leaving me unburned.

The neurological components supporting this simplified internal model of the external world is essentially a switching mechanism that triggers or does not trigger motor activity. If the pattern of sensory input that enters the system matches the internal model, the motor neurons are activated and movement takes place. If not, no movement takes place.

Even in simple situations, however, such as the task of picking up the iron, there are more than two choices involved. Different locations of the iron, different positions of the iron, and different starting points of my arm relative to the iron dramatically increase the number of choices of approach movements that are possible. To trigger the effective motor activity my internal model, which is an aggregate of expectancy, need not be sensitive to sensory information representing all of those possibilities. When the motor activity occurs, my internal model has served its purpose. More often than not, through the use of my internal model, I do behave effectively.

For my brain to have performed these functions, I must have two basic system functions. My brain must be able to coordinate goal-directed behavior and to make internal representations of external occurrences. Based upon what is known about the anatomy and bio-chemical functioning of the neuron, what is the basic neuron-configuration that would make possible goal-directed behavior and internal representations of external reality? Sommerhoff noted that, although the central nervous system is capable of both digital and analogue functioning, and the actual manner in which the neurons may interact is far more complex than he would depict in his simple system, for the purpose of demonstrating logically the possibilities manifest in neuron-configurations, it was only necessary for him to assume a digital functioning of neurons. That is to say, it was only necessary to assume that the incoming signal would be strong enough to activate a neuron, or it would not.

Sommerhoff asked himself the question, "What neurological components and configurations of these components would make possible such an internal model of the external world?" His theoretical answer to this question is the "lambda system." Sommerhoff's **lambda system** is "...*any network of neurons in which (i) a number of input channels are shared by all excitatory neurons of the network; (ii) the excitatory neurons are subject to some form of recurring or forward inhibition with a lateral spread which favors those that are most receptive to the given pattern of* *input; (iii) some or all of the synapses of the shared input channels can undergo lasting changes as the result of experience."*

Sommerhoff then goes on the demonstrate that it is logically possible for his lambda system configuration to explain the human capacity for learning, recognition, reproduction of temporal sequences, memory, imagination, recognition of properties, and the recognition of relationships. Sommerhoff states that there is some empirical evidence for the existence of cell assemblies similar to those depicted by his lambda system. But he does not insist that such neuron assemblies must actually account for higher mental functioning. Rather, he has described a system that may give comfort to the reasoning person *that it is possible* for what is known about the neurophysiology of the brain to account for higher mental functioning.

This is not to say that the great thoughts and creative expressions of the human race are merely the summation of the occurrence or lack of occurrence of neuron excitation. Rather, based upon relatively simple neuronal structures, the *complex* integration of these structures may *possibly* account for these supreme human experiences.

Beginning with simple lambda systems, these supreme human experiences are possible because of the ever-increasing complexity in the integration of the central nervous system. For such higher mental functioning to occur, this integration is not merely between the cells within a lambda assembly but between cells and lambda systems throughout the various functionally differentiated components of the brain.

Higher Mental Functions

Extrapolating from Sommerhoff's *Logic of the Living Brain,* let us consider how, with ever-increasing integration of the central nervous system, such higher mental functioning as consciousness and reasoning may have occurred. Let us assume that "ontogeny recapitulates phylogeny." As this saying indicates, individual human development, from the embryo to maturity, follows a pattern similar to that of the evolution from simple cells to complex higher mammals. Likewise, the development of the central nervous system of the individual follows a pattern similar to that of the evolution of the brains of reptiles, to simple mammals, and from simple mammals to primates. The partially developed human being, still in the uterus, has a brain that allows it to perform some of the vegetative functions performed by the reptile. Like the reptile, this underdeveloped human has a central nervous system that enables it to experience pain and discomfort and also the absence of such feelings. As the individual human being continues to develop, its brain acquires a **limbic system** and an allocortex. Like primitive mammals, this somewhat more developed human being may be capable of experiencing a wider variety of feelings than reptiles and may be motivated by these feelings to act in somewhat less ritualistic manners.

Prior to birth, the human being has a fully developed neocortex, and the primary pathways interconnecting the various components of the neonate brain have developed. The intrauterine experiential environment, however, is a relatively impoverished environment, and the integration of the various components of the brain, from within lambda systems to between the major structural components of the neuroanatomy, is relatively unintegrated. This human being, nonetheless, is far more capable than the reptile or the primitive mammal of storing and integrating information. Let us trace what may be occurring soon after this relatively unintegrated organism enters the far more complex postnatal environment. It is not known whether the newborn is suddenly assaulted by an overwhelming barrage of sensations or whether nature has desensitized the child temporarily to enable it to survive the birth "trauma." In either case, there must come a time when a great many kinds of sensory stimulation are impinging upon the infant. If the central nervous system of the infant is an all-bands receiver, the infant's brain would be one mass of activated neurons. Whatever coordinating capacities this newborn brain might have would surely be overwhelmed by this cacophony of stimulation. Fortunately, the brain seems to have built-in dampeners. For the brain to process incoming information, it must first be aroused. In the healthy intact-infant, a biochemical environment will exist within and surrounding the neurons of the limbic system, particularly the reticular formation, that will allow the reticular formation to send activating stimulation to the neocortex. A different biochemical environment within the limbic system, caused by inadequate nourishment, exhaustion, or disease, would inhibit this reticular formation stimulation of the neocortex. The former state would be arousal, and the latter state would be sleep or unconsciousness.

The reticular formation stimulation is a general stimulation of the neocortex. Signals coming from another part of the limbic system, from the hippocampus and the amygdaloid, are more specific in their arousal effects upon the neocortex. This limbic system activation is capable of reinforcing a specific incoming neural activity, or ongoing neural activity, within the neocortex. This limbic system activation allows the newborn infant to attend to specific sensations. Within the limbic system, attention is apparently moderated by the current drive state of the individual. As biochemical information travels through the bloodstream to the hypothalamus, information is received about the deficit or excess of stimulation in specific parts of the body. At this early stage in the development of the child, the coordination of the drive state in the limbic system's attentional capacity is likely to focus attention on sensory input from such channels, as the aroused central nervous system of the infant focuses on the sensations associated with the warmth, wetness, and malleability of the mother's breasts. The neocortex may be very little involved in the control and coordination of the muscles that are activated as a result of this arousal and focused attention. But the reptile-like functioning of the cerebellum is likely to enable the newborn infant to accomplish the task of sucking the breast.

Very little time elapses, however, before the infant accomplishes a more effective integration of all of these and some additional components of its central nervous system. Now, when the drive state is one of deprivation of nourishment, the infant may become aroused, and the limbic excitation of the neocortex may involve expressions of discomfort, through crying, a visual searching for the breast, flailing and then groping of the arms and hands, and in a much more vigorous sucking and head-butting activity. This complex of the central nervous system excitation and coordinated muscular activity is likely to be more effective in providing nourishment and, therefore, in moderating the drive state and in increasing the probability of survival of the infant. This is another illustration of the general principle that the increase in the integration of an organization increases the probability of the maintenance of that organization.

Forming Internal Representations

Just when it occurs is not known, but sometime during the development of this increasing integration of the central nervous system of an infant, the infant becomes capable of forming internal representations of the external world. Within the various parts of the neocortex, cells or cell assemblies such as lambda systems, are changed by the incoming sensory excitation, first within the synaptic structure and perhaps later within the DNA of the neuron, so that the cell configuration has a heightened sensitivity to a specific pattern of previously experienced stimulation. It need not be the exact pattern of stimulation that is incoming, but it must be enough like the pattern to which the cell assembly is sensitized to activate that cell-assembly. When that particular cell-assembly in combination with cell-assemblies being similarly stimulated in other parts of the neocortex is activated, the related motor activity is activated. This activation of the motor functioning of the infant may be accomplished without that which we might call consciousness. It is merely the functioning of a highly integrated system—as a complex pattern of incoming stimulation triggers a complex pattern of neural organization, which directly stimulates a complex pattern of motor behavior. At the same time as this external stimulation/central nervous system stimulation/motor activity cycle is occurring, this activation of the neocortex is supported by drive state arousal and attentional excitation impinging upon the neocortex from the limbic system. The sensation/neocortex/coordination/motor-behavior cycle of excitation is, in fact, supported in its continued firing by the neural reverberation of excitation between the neocortex and the limbic system. If the limbic system component of this neural chain discontinues its functioning, the motor activity would cease.

But other channels of reverberation are possible. With some degree of arousal and attention activation from the limbic system, with or without supportive arousal from the drive system, reverberation may take place within the neocortex. The same cell-assembly that was coordinating the sucking activity might now be stimulated in the absence of incoming sensation. Such reverberation within the neocortex is what Sommerhoff supposes to be the internal representation of external experience. It may also be thought of as a primitive form of imagery.

Imagery *is the generic term for all forms of storage and activation of higher mental functioning.* Visual images, thoughts, patterns of sound, and patterns of sensations are all forms of imagery. Imagery may be stimulated by incoming sensation or by the excitation of the external or internal sense modalities, or imagery may be stimulated by limbic system drive states and by attentional excitation. Imagery may occur under various levels of reticular formation arousal, from heightened general awareness to the low level of reticular arousal usually associated with dreaming.

But what is the function of these internal representations of the external world? As these internal representations have been described to this point, they are merely **epiphenomenal**, or *byproducts of neural excitation that will be ongoing whether or not this phenomenon called* *internal representation is occurring.* These internal representations can only have a function if they combine with other internal representations to form more complex, more highly integrated representations that may then effect something else within the system, either behavior or other internal representations. This, of course, is a description of thought and imagination.

But before we can be comfortable with this explanation of imagery, a number of other important questions must be answered. What motivates imagery? What directs imagery?

Why should an internal representation excite or combine with another specific internal representations rather than with internal representations at random?

Here is my thinking. For an immature, relatively unintegrated human being, living in a hypothetical demand-free environment, there would be no motivation for imagery to occur. Under the urgings of drive excitation from the limbic system, readily available sensory input would trigger existing lambda systems, and motor behavior would occur to satisfy the drive. But even the most overly solicitous parent cannot immediately satisfy all of an infant's needs. Frustration of a drive would trigger another limbic system excitation, a feeling that we might label hyper-alertness, fear, or anxiety. Under the urgings of this feeling, motor behavior becomes random, and likewise there may be a random firing of lambda systems in the neocortex. Two things may now occur. The random motor behavior may chance upon an activity that will initiate drive-reduction. Or, it is more likely that a lambda system in the neocortex that has previously been associated with the pleasurable feeling of drive-reduction will be excited. The motor behavior triggered by this randomly excited lambda system might serve no function, but the associated pleasurable feeling will temporarily reduce the anxiety. Therefore, in time, the excitation of imagery will come to have its own purpose—the reduction of anxiety.

This hypothesized process may be summarized as follows: When there is failure in the automatic satisfaction of a drive, anxiety increases. Under the urging of anxiety, the neocortex is stimulated to produce imagery. The motor behavior associated with this imagery is, for the most part, nonfunctional and tends to lessen. Imagery that in the past has been associated with unpleasant, non neutral excitation from the limbic system is inhibited by the attentional excitation of the limbic system, and those lambda systems images that are associated with pleasurable limbic system excitation are enhanced by further attentional excitation from the limbic system. Therefore, a specific image is activated that at least temporarily reduces the discomfort caused by the frustrated drive.

The unsatisfied drive, however, soon reasserts itself, and the process is repeated. This results in a sequencing of images, a sequencing that is as yet unrelated to the external world. But during this time, the affective state of the organism is sufficiently ameliorated so that the neocortex is not overly stimulated, and random excessive motor behavior is not occurring. There is now more time for the moderated motor behavior to chance upon activity that moves the infant toward drive-reduction.

Imagery has now come to have two independent functions. It reduces anxiety, and it makes more effective problem-solving possible. In time, the sequencing of images is refined and more directly related to the sequencing of motor behavior that leads to drive-reducing activity. *Behavior that solves problems in the external world is said to be* "**rational behavior.**" *The sequence of images that triggers this rational behavior may be termed* "**rational thought.**" In time, rational thought, because it leads to problem-solving rational behavior, will come to be pleasurable. Moreover, even random images that have in the past been associated with pleasurable limbic system excitation, as well as the rational sequencing of imagery associated with rational drive-reducing behavior, will come to be pleasurable.

The kind of imagery characteristically produced by the developing human being will be related to the frequency of occurrence of such successful problem-solving. Children who solve more problems through the use of rational imagery might tend to indulge in more intentional imagery. Children who are less effective with the use of rational imagery might tend to daydream more.

An environment that is rich in challenges that the child can master, challenges that stimulate all of the sense modalities and, therefore, simulate all areas of the neocortex, is an environment that will stimulate more and more complex sequences and combinations of images. This will result in a greater integration of the central nervous system, and in a more effective integration of the central nervous system—and, therefore, in more effective problem solving. The capacity for developing integrated imagery is another step in the development of the individual and in the evolution of the species toward the more effective maintenance of the organization.

Therefore, the more integrated organism is one that begins with the anatomical capacity for neurophysiological integration, one that has developed further integration of the lambda systems of the neocortex and the subcortical limbic system, and one that is motivated by limbic system excitation to indulge in imagery that is not necessarily related to *immediate* motor behavior problem-solving. Image making then becomes a self-motivating activity of more integrated organisms, such as humans. Who knows, perhaps other animals are also blessed with the pleasurable habit of image making.

This indulgence in image making is more than just pleasure producing, however, it is highly functional. When a "rational" sequencing of lambda systems has been learned, a series of images or a series of problem-solving behaviors or motor behaviors can occur very rapidly with a minimum of neocortex activation. For example, when a diver is to execute a complicated dive, the lambda systems containing the internal representations of the name of that dive might be all the neocortical activation that is needed to initiate and coordinate the elaborate sequence of overlearned motor behaviors that is the actual dive.

Neurophysiological Motivation

But in new situations, in which the next step in the behavioral sequence or the next image is not already learned, why is one lambda system activated rather than any other lambda system?

To answer this question it is necessary to elaborate on the motivation of highly integrated organisms. Under the urgings of a need or drive, which is to say, under the urgings of activation of certain parts of the limbic system, there is general arousal or activation of the neocortex. There may also be attentional arousal or heightened arousal of certain areas of the neocortex that have a learned association with activation originating from specific need-related areas of the limbic system. Activation of integrated components of the central system comes to have a learned association with problem-solving and need-gratification. Therefore, the integrated functioning of the central nervous system may activate the pleasure centers within the limbic system. Such integrated functioning at least does not activate fear or anxiety centers in the limbic system. On the other hand, increased general arousal of the neocortex without integrated functioning has a learned association with unsatisfied needs or threats to the organization of the organism. The general arousal of activation by the reticular formation and the attentional arousal from the amygdala function is in opposition to one another. The attentional arousal enables an increased activation of specific neocortex lambda systems by suppressing all other areas of neocortex activation. If the pattern of neural activation emanating from the lambda system that is currently being aroused by the need activation and facilitated by the arousal activation is capable of activating another lambda system, the arousal of this new lambda system will occur and therefore, by definition, the next image will occur. When there is no learned sequencing of lambda systems, it is likely that there will be numerous lambda systems that are subsequently activated. But it is the integrated functioning of the central nervous system that has in the past led to a decrease in overall neocortical arousal or disorganization. Therefore, only one lambda system will actually be activated. If this newly activated lambda system triggers behavior or an image that either satisfies the need or had been associated with past anxiety-reduction, then the limbic system attentional and general arousal activation will lessen. General arousal of the neocortex will continue at a level that will allow random pleasurable images to occur. Since the attentional arousal is not narrowing the ordering of lambda systems to only those that will be activated by the previous lambda system, new, previously unassociated sequencings of lambda systems can occur. These will not, however, be totally unrelated lambda systems. Rather, they will be lambda systems that are *generally* less related than those that may occur under the urgings of the narrowing attentional activation from the limbic system. The wider spectrum of possible lambda system pairings increases the probability that new pairings will occur that will make possible novel problem-solving motor behaviors or anxiety-reducing images. In either case, under heightened or moderated general arousal of the neocortex, the activation in sequence of one lambda system by another is accompanied by a temporary reduction of the attentional activation excitation from the limbic system. *It is this instance, when the central nervous system changes from non-integration to reintegration, this instance when the organization of the central nervous system changes from a state of relative peril to relative security that is the current apex of the organization of the organism. When we define the concept of self, we will come to describe this moment as a moment of* **consciousness.**

Even Further Integration of the Central Nervous System

But who or what is directing this elaborate sequencing of images and behavior? The answer, of course, is no one. The form of this question would once again throw us into the problem of infinite regression, that is, "Who is directing the director?" To understand concepts and experiences such as consciousness and the self, and yet avoid infinite regression, it is necessary to further elaborate on the concept of the integration of the central nervous system.

We have been discussing the activation of one lambda system by another as though these were linear occurrences. There might be simple lambda systems made up of one neuron activating another neuron, but such systems are probably a rarity in the human central nervous system. The kind of lambda systems that coordinate motor behavior and that the are models of the internal representation of reality that we have come to term images are most likely elaborately complex and made up of hundreds of thousands of neurons interacting in astronomical numbers of synapses. Moreover, when these elaborate lambda systems successfully activate another lambda system, changes take place in the new lambda system, first at the synapses and perhaps later within the DNA, that join these two lambda systems into an even more complex integration. As a matter of fact, the tendency of the central nervous system, under the general activation of the reticular formation, is toward total activation of the neocortex. That is to say, when the organism is not asleep or unconscious, there tends to be a low level of activation of all of the neurons in the neocortex. As the intensity of general activation increases, those neurons that are integrated into the total integration of the neocortex become more activated than those neurons that are not involved in the total integration of the neocortex. This is apparently accomplished by the supportive reverberation that occurs among integrated neurons within the neocortex. In a mature human being, when a pattern of stimulation activates the nerve endings of sense modalities, and this complex pattern of neuronal activation reaches the central nervous system and triggers a complex lambda system that is sensitive to that pattern of externally stimulated neuronal activity, then an internal representation or image occurs. If there is an existing learned motor behavior associated with this activated lambda system then this behavior automatically occurs, and some degree of effective behavior takes place. When a novel pattern of externally stimulated neuronal activity reaches the central nervous system, and there is no lambda system available to be activated by that novel pattern of stimulation, the central nervous system is to some degree disorganized. This activates the reticular formation to increase the general level of arousal, which results in an increase in the number of lambda systems involved in the total integration of the central nervous system. This makes available a greater number of lambda systems, one or more of which might then be activated by the novel incoming stimulation.

Not all novel incoming stimulation increases the general arousal of the neocortex. If the incoming stimulation is too novel, totally beyond the experience of the organism, even though it is stimulating the sense modalities to some degree, the organism might not respond to it as a pattern but merely as part of the random external stimulation that is always present in the organism's environment. Only when some component of that pattern causes stimulation to become so intense that the organism must respond to that familiar intensity will the central nervous system have available a lambda system that will be activated by the intense incoming stimulation. Then there may be no learned lambda system motor sequence to cope with this intense stimulation, but there will be a learned association or lambda system coordinating the intensity of the external stimulation with the drive areas of the limbic system. This will result in a heightened general arousal of the neocortex activation of attentional arousal from the amygdala. The motor behavior associated with this arousal of the attentional activation of the neocortex is a focusing of the sense modalities on the source of stimulation. Or, if the source is not readily apparent, the motor behavior is a general pattern of motor behavior that may be described as a search pattern, one that increases the likelihood of focusing on the source of excessive stimulation. Once this focusing is accomplished, there is an increased probability that the greater information afforded by the focusing will present a pattern of excitation to the central nervous system that will activate an existing lambda system.

If even this process fails to result in a lambda system activation that will coordinate motor behavior to reduce the intensity of the stimulation then attentional activation as well as general activation intensifies. The increase spiraling of this activation might result in random aggressive movements, flight, panic, or fainting. This disorganization of the central nervous system by excessive stimulation is intolerable.

Most effective problem-solving occurs when the attentional activation is strong enough to coordinate effective focusing and when the general activation of the neocortex is great enough to make available a large percentage of the integrated neocortex. This allows the rapid sequencing of relatively related images. As each image activates a subsequent relatively related image there is that moment of reintegration that temporarily reduces the attentional activation and allows a broader spectrum of available lambda systems or images so that the next relatively related image can be activated. This rapidly occurring process makes possible a refining of the images, or patterns of lambda systems, to more accurately fit the incoming pattern of stimulation. When there is a close enough fit between the pattern of external stimulation and the excitability pattern of this newly created lambda system then a motor behavior may be activated that has a higher probability of coping with the intense external stimulation.

As an illustration of this complex and interactive central nervous system activity consider the following. You are asleep in your bed when a mosquito whines by your ear. Without being fully aroused from your sleep, you attempt to brush away the mosquito. A learned lambda system was available to coordinate the incoming stimulation with the appropriate motor behavior.

Later, however, a novel low-level intensity stimulation occurs near your ear. This stimulation is too low to arouse a generalized fear response from the limbic system, and there is no available lambda system in the neocortex to coordinate motor behavior. Although your sense modalities *were* activated by this low level of external stimulation, the pattern of stimulation does not register in your neocortex, and therefore you do not react.

Then, suddenly, the intensity of noise increases, but there is still no central nervous system lambda system that is activated by this pattern of incoming stimulation. However, the intensity is such that a generalized fear response is activated, and you are aroused from your sleep. In the darkness, you try to focus on the source of the novel sound. The focusing tells you that the sound emanates from near your head, and the lambda system currently activated in your more generally aroused neocortex tentatively identifies the pattern as that associated with a woman's screaming! There should be no other person in your bed! But instead of panicking, you are now even more aroused, and your integrated central nervous system activates the lambda system that coordinates turning on the light. Your more effective focusing now centers in on the small object on the wall near your head. This clear pattern of incoming stimulation activates an existing lambda system that is associated with a low level of anxiety in its learned connection with the limbic system, and you immediately begin to relax. You recognize the small tree frog that has blundered into your room. Though the sound you heard is similar to a woman's screaming, thank goodness there is no screaming woman in your bed.

This illustration may make clear the more abstract description of what was occurring in the central nervous system. But notice, in order to clarify what was occurring in your central nervous system, I had to talk about you—I had to talk about your "self." The self is a convenient explanatory concept, but surely the self is more than just a concept. To explore this issue we must move beyond Gerd Sommerhoff's neuro-physiological speculation onto the psychological level of speculation. It is now time to begin our understanding of the self.

And the Self Begins to Function

Understanding the Self

The self is many things, and therefore there is much confusion in our understanding of the self. In the most general sense, the self is either a concept or an experience. The concept of self is a way in which we organize our thinking about the ways we behave and the reasons we behave in those ways. But the self is also an experience. It is the immediate awareness of our thoughts and our feelings. A useful theory of self-development, a clear and relatively simple way of thinking about ourselves, would give us a greater feeling of certainty that what we are experiencing as ourselves is both a useful concept and a meaningful experience.

Here is what I propose. **"The self"** *is a series of levels of integration of the central nervous system.* These levels of the self are:

1. The Affective or Limbic-Self
2. The Content or Cerebral-Self
3. The Invested-Self
4. The Functional-Self or Consciousness
5. The Self-Aware-Self
6. The Self-Concepts-Self
7. The Integrated-Self
8. The Transcendent-Self

The self did not evolve phylogenetically, and could not develop ontogenetically, until the many biochemical processes and anatomical components of the human central nervous system came into being. But it is the *integration* of these processes and components that is the self.

MacLean's (1974) concept of the triune brain is a convenient way of categorizing the major anatomical components of the human brain. A vegetative form of physical existence might be sustained by the coordinated functioning of the reptilian and mammalian components of the human brain, but there would be no self without the neocortex. Even the addition of a neocortex to complete the triune brain does not automatically create a self. The self is developed only through experience and learning and when the limbic system has aroused the neocortex. Until arousal of the neocortex, the self exists only as potential. The limbic system can do no arousing without the vegetative functions that are coordinated, to a large extent, by the reptilian brain. In other words, *the self can exist only through a high level of integration of the many components of the human brain, and all of these components and the necessary integration are not present in the reptilian brain.*

The Affective or Limbic-Self

In addition to the general and attentional arousal of the neocortex, which occurs when its components are activated, the limbic system also appears to be the anatomical locus of all of our feelings. **The Affective or "Limbic-Self"** *is the psychological conceptualization of this limbic system function.* Research has demonstrated that direct electrical stimulation of areas of the hypothalamus, the hippocampus, and the amygdala are experienced as such basic feelings as anger, fear, and pleasure. There are even areas of the limbic system that when stimulated result in the subjects' reporting such feelings as interest, affection, ecstasy, and a general feeling of knowing or understanding without specification of that which is known or understood. In other words, it appears that there might be areas in the limbic system that, when activated, could be experienced as *any* feeling that we are able to identify, that is, when the it is associated with activation of the neocortex.

Feelings motivate and direct motor behavior, and feelings also motivate and direct imagery. But the activation of these limbic system areas is a part of an integrated neural process. When excessive and therefore noxious external stimulation activates the neocortex, or when a pattern of external stimulation activates a lambda system that is associated with a past experience of such a noxious stimulus, these motivational neurons or neuron assemblies in the limbic system are activated. This limbic system activation reverberates with the neocortex to continue activation of the already aroused lambda systems and to activate other related lambda systems. All of this activation then coordinates behavior to defend against the threat. Even when the threat is internal, as in the case of a biochemical change in the blood impinging upon the hypothalamus, the hypothalamus, in turn, activates other areas of the limbic system, which in turn might activate the neocortex.

This defensive activation of the limbic system may occur without involvement of the self, as might most of the behaviors that are effective in maintaining the organization of the organism. This is because there is no affect or feeling associated with limbic system activation unless there is sufficient integration of this limbic system activation with associate activation of the neocortex. The lowest level of self, the Affective or Limbic-Self, only exists when limbic system activation activates the neocortex and some form of imagery occurs. Otherwise, the limbic system is merely the repository of potential feelings. The Limbic-Self exists and *is* functioning when you say that you feel something. But you cannot say or be aware that you feel something without the activation of neocortex. Therefore, there is no pure or exclusive functioning of the limbic system as the Limbic-Self. The closest we may come to pure functioning of an exclusive limbic system Limbic-Self would be in such artificial states as those experimental conditions in which the limbic system receives direct electrical stimulation from the experimenter, or when drugs are administered that have direct effect on the limbic system, or when areas of the limbic system have been damaged, or in hypnotic or dream states. In these unusual states, the feelings may be powerful, and may even bring about lasting and perhaps dysfunctional changes in the personality, since the feelings are insufficiently or inappropriately integrated with cerebral cortex imagery. But usually, these Limbic-Self states are merely vague and short-lived. More often than not, there might be a feeling that something important or relevant has occurred but what that something is cannot be understood or remembered.

The Limbic-Self functions at a lower level of central nervous system integration than levels of the self yet to be described, but the Limbic-Self is nevertheless one of our experiences of self. More important, the Limbic-Self is an essential component in the development of more integrated levels of self.

The Content or Cerebral-Self

The exact anatomical location of the various feelings in the limbic system differs from individual to individual and may differ within individuals from time to time. Information may be stored in the limbic system through genetic coding and probably through experience and learning. But the neocortex, and more specifically the cerebral cortex, is by far a greater storehouse of information needed for human survival and thriving. In the human being, the cerebral cortex is proportionately the largest area of the brain. It also contains the greatest number and variety of neurons, and its potential for information storage is enormous. **The Content or Cerebral-Self** *is all of this stored information.* Just as with the Limbic-Self, the Cerebral-Self does not normally exist in a pure state. The Cerebral-Self must be integrated with and activated by the limbic system. Until activated by the limbic system, the Cerebral-Self exists only as potential as, for example, when you are unconscious or in deep sleep. At low levels of limbic system activation of the cerebral cortex, the Cerebral-Self functions as a vast variety of pre-wired neuronal interrelations available to be activated by specific patterns of incoming afferent neuronal activation. As limbic system activation and integration between the limbic system and the cerebral cortex increases, more of these neuronal patterns are made available, and the number and complexity of the interconnection of these patterns increases. Therefore, your **Cerebral-Self** *is your storehouse of all the information you have about your world, and your self, and your self in the world.* As your peripheral nervous system registers patterns of stimulation, the information or patterns available for excitation stored in your Cerebral-Self are selected to be activated to coordinate motor behavior or to activate related and relevant imagery. The capacity of your neocortex, and therefore of your Cerebral-Self, to store information and to add to the store through learning increases your capacity for survival. As living organisms evolve in complexity of integration, their survival capacity increases. The human central nervous system, with its proportionately larger cerebrum, apparently has the most integrated central nervous system of all living organisms. The human being's capacity to respond flexibly and creatively to an ever-changing environment is a result of this highly integrated central nervous system, and it is this flexibility and creativity in response to the environment that gives the human being, we hope, the highest *potential* for survival of all living creatures.

Perhaps all mammals have a Limbic-Self. They appear to have an immediate awareness of their feelings. Probably all more highly developed mammals have a Cerebral-Self. Such mammals have the capacity to store and process information and learning experiences. But perhaps only human beings and other primates have the capacity for the more integrated levels of the self.

The Invested-Self

The content of the Cerebral-Self is information, but the term information needs elaboration. This information consists of all the predictions one can "generally" make about how the world will respond to one's self-induced movements, or how one will react, think, and feel in response to one's actions and thoughts. These predictions are generalizations; and these generalizations are the natural inclination of the central nervous system. Sommerhoff calls these **generalizations**, *"directive correlations." Since it would be impossible for the central nervous system to have a cell assembly or lambda system for every internal representation of every aspect of the external world, lambda systems are usually activated by a range of patterns and not by just one specific pattern.* For example, if I toss a ball into the air, based on the amount of effort and the direction that I give to the ball, I would expect it to fall back to the ground in a certain area. I would not be surprised if it fell anywhere within that two or three foot radius. But if it fell ten feet away, I would be startled. Ten feet would be beyond the range of predictions contained within my internal representation of the external world. This tendency to create simple directive correlations or generalizations about external reality is not acquired through experience. It is not a mental or verbal activity. Rather, according to Sommerhoff, it is a by-product of the manner in which neurons relate to neurons to create lambda systems.

As the individual matures, however, more generalizations are made through the use of language, which is a step beyond this natural property of lambda systems. Such "concept formations" occur from the interrelation of lambda systems without immediate reference to the external world. This process will be described later.

The content or Cerebral-Self of adult human beings is the primary locus of simple generalization, as in expectations of where the ball should fall, and of very complex concepts adult humans have about their experiences, as in how and by whom they expect to be loved. But the limbic system is also involved with all knowledge, predictions, or concepts contained in the Cerebral-Self. There is no purely cognitive, non-affective experience. At the very least, no thought may occur without some degree of limbic system induced arousal. But one of the most pervasive feelings emanating from the limbic system is the feeling of "familiarity." **Familiarity** *is a feeling associated with having one's predictions about one's self and one's world come true.* It is the ball falling where the ball is supposed to fall. Another common feeling is some degree of **unfamiliarity**. It is the ball falling ten feet away. **Familiarity and unfamiliarity** *are actually a continuum of feelings that range from the feeling of belonging, or exactly like me, to a fearful feeling of awe that something is totally uncanny or otherworldly and certainly not like me.* In between, there might be the feeling of, "This is more or less me, but so what."

By definition then, *the* **Invested-Self** *consists of all those predictions about the world, and how the body will respond to the world, that are associated with the feeling of belonging.* Just how familiar such information has to be to be experienced as "belongingness" and therefore to be included in the Invested-Self varies from individual to individual. But whatever is within this range of accepted familiarity is the Invested-Self, and whatever falls outside of this range of familiarity is experienced as "not self."

On the neurophysiological level, the feeling of belonging associated with mentation about the self is an indication that *Invested-Self* lambda systems are complex or more integrated than most other Cerebral-Self lambda systems. This greater complexity of the Invested-Self lambda systems allows finer discriminations between incoming stimulation, some of which are experienced as various degrees of Invested-Self and most as not Invested-Self.

In addition to the pervasive feeling of familiarity, information within the Invested-Self may be associated with any feeling, and not all of these feelings are positive. You may predict that when you make overtures to a person of the opposite sex you will be rejected. The feeling associated with this prospect of rejection may be acute embarrassment and self-loathing. But, nevertheless, these predictions and these unpleasant feelings are a part of your Invested-Self.

A major component of the Invested-Self is the **body schema.** As arousal or activation by the limbic system or the cerebral cortex increases, the cerebral cortex is bombarded by information from all of the external sense modalities, and also from the internal sense modalities. Nerve endings from all over the body tell of the body's temperature, its relative comfort or discomfort, its position in space, and even its changing reactions to atmospheric pressure and gravity. Most of this information is so familiar as to go unnoticed most of the time. When asked how you feel, you generally respond with a description of an emotion and not with a description of the various simple sensations that constitute the body schema. Only when something is wrong with the body, when the excitation from some part of the body is generating a decidedly unfamiliar feeling from the limbic system, do you attend to the body schema. Such "unfamiliar" information about the body schema is usually not a part of the Invested-Self. The exception to this rule is chronic illness or dysfunction and even chronic pain. We may come to accept such abnormal conditions of the body schema as a part of the Invested-Self if our Invested-Self also contains the prediction that we have no other choice.

As has been said, the Invested-Self is a part of the content of the Cerebral-Self, but it represents a higher level of integration of the central nervous system than the Cerebral-Self. As usual, the function of this increased integration of the central nervous system is to improve efficiency in the survival efforts of the human organism. Compared to the Invested-Self lambda systems, the less integrated Cerebral-Self lambda systems are able to respond to a wider variety of incoming stimulation. They are less complex, and therefore there are fewer components that must generally "fit." Early in my maturation I might have felt comfortable with the ball's falling within a wider radius, but not so wide that I was discouraged from trying to catch the ball I had tossed in the air. My more mature Invested-Self lambda systems, being more complex, would generate a more limited range of expectations. The ball must fall *almost* exactly where I expect it to fall. Put another way, my more complex Invested-Self lambda system leads me to expect aspects of my Invested-Self to be *just* like I expect them to be—or I get upset. If I am a professional baseball player, I *expect* a fly ball to fall into my glove, or I'm disgusted with myself. On the positive side, my more integrated Invested-Self makes me hyper-alert to events that might change the organization of my Invested-Self, and thus my more integrated Invested-Self better enables me protect my self-organization. The next time, I focus intensely on the fly ball, and I make certain that I catch it.

Now that I am aroused by the onset of a stimulus that might disrupt the organization that is my Invested-Self, what am I to do about it? After all, there was no automatic motor response or mentation available to take care of the threat or I would not have become uncomfortably aroused in the first place. The answer is the development of an even more integrated level of the self—the Functional-Self, or consciousness. In other words, I couldn't have decided to focus on that next fly ball coming in my direction unless I first became conscious of what had happened, that I had missed a fly ball I expected to catch.

The Functional-Self or Consciousness

Do we really have consciousness? This is an age-old philosophical question that most laymen might think absurd. Laymen are familiar with the feeling of being aware of what is happening around them and also of being aware that they are aware of what is happening. But philosophers have long argued that it is unnecessary to posit a concept such as consciousness to explain human behavior. They argued that the central nervous system may be capable of *automatically* processing all incoming information and eventually arriving at sufficiently efficient and effective coping behavior. In observing other people's behavior, philosophers could come up with no irrefutable evidence these other people were experiencing this thing we call consciousness. Furthermore, even though these philosophers might not have denied that *they* themselves experienced this thing called consciousness, they questioned whether it has any function. Perhaps it is just **epiphenomenal,** or *a byproduct of the automatic problem-solving occurring within the central nervous system.* It is a shadow of the real that has no effect upon the real. Moreover, there is our old question of infinite regression. Who or what is within the self that is being conscious of consciousness?

To feel comfortable with the concept of consciousness it will be necessary to carefully define the term, to establish its function, and to avoid the problem of infinite regression. But before defining consciousness, let's be sure we can agree that all effectively functioning adults are capable of another pervasive limbic system feeling, the feeling of recognition. **Recognition** *is the first moment of experiencing the feeling of familiarity; it is the "ah ha" experience of, I know that!* But being merely a limbic system feeling it has no content. It exists merely as a feeling of knowing without knowing what one knows.

So what now is consciousness? **Consciousness** *is that moment of synthesis of the Invested-Self and the limbic system when the feeling of recognition is activated within the limbic system in association with a cell assembly in the neocortex.* In other words, consciousness is occurring when the feeling of recognition is associated with an image, or a word, a scene, or a sound stored in the neocortex. The moment that I recognize some words I have just written (sirloin steak, for instance), I experience the feeling of recognition as well as other feelings associated with those words, but I also picture the words, or what the words labels, or I hear the words, or I even taste the words, all of which are images stored in my neocortex.

However, consciousness, being a synthesis, is more than the sum of its parts. Like water, which is more than just hydrogen and oxygen, consciousness has properties not contained in its parts. Just like water, consciousness can do things that its parts cannot. It has more effective functions than its individual parts.

The Function of Consciousness   Consciousness or the Functional-Self is a needed next step in the continuing development of the self. When an unfamiliar pattern of stimulation is incompatible with the organization of the central nervous system and demands attention, this unfamiliar pattern is a "problem" and requires "problem-solving." *Consciousness evolved to assist in this problem-solving.* When attentional activation is directed from the limbic system to the cerebral cortex, the result is a heightened focusing on the source of disruptive stimulation. Even though there is a corresponding increase in the overall stimulation of the cerebral cortex, this heightened focusing is primarily a narrowing of stimulation, which inhibits and makes less available other areas of the cerebral cortex. As a result, the next and more effective functioning level of the Functional-Self, sequential mentation, may be inhibited. **Sequential Mentation** *is the sequencing of one moment of consciousness after another.* For the process of sequential mentation to occur there must be a release from the narrow focusing caused by excessive focusing on a threat. Otherwise the focusing would continue unabated, since no only partially similar but potential problem solving lambda systems can be triggered. In other words, when there is no neuron assembly that is sensitive to the unfamiliar pattern of incoming stimulation, and therefore no automatic coping behavior can occur, there would be no reduction in arousal. Since the "threat" continues, there would be an increase in attentional and focusing activation from the limbic system, along with more intense arousal, and that would further inhibit problem-solving rather than facilitate it.

More effective consciousness *can* occur, however and, more often than not, it does. Remember, the brain does not store exact internal models of the external world. Rather, each of these lambda systems, or internal models, is a generalization about the external world. Therefore, the unfamiliar external stimulation activates a great many relatively similar internal models. An internal model that is at least somewhat *dissimilar* to the unfamiliar stimulation may then be activated. While this activated internal model might not solve the problem presented by the unfamiliar stimulation, it nevertheless activates a feeling in the limbic system that I have labeled, "**recognition**." *This feeling is associated with a relative increase in the integration of the central nervous system, a relative increase in the organization of the organism and a reduction in arousal intensity, and this enables a temporary reduction in the focusing mode of the cerebral cortex.* This reduction in focusing temporarily disinhibits the other areas of the cerebral cortex and allows the new combination of relatively less unfamiliar internal stimulation to activate the relatively similar lambda systems. The new set of lambda systems is being activated not only by the familiar stimulation but by this stimulation in combination with the first lambda system that was activated. When this next lambda system is activated, there is another moment of recognition, and the process proceeds until an original integration occurs in the central nervous system, one that never before existed, but one that might be capable of activating motor behavior that will cope with the unfamiliar stimulation.

This process, which has been described in quasi-neurophysiological terms, is of course the *psychological* process of thinking. **Thinking** *is the common term for a form of sequential mentation, and may be the sequencing of not only words but also scenes, sounds, or smell, etc.* Therefore, **consciousness** *is a synthesis, an integration between the limbic system and the cerebral cortex, that allows one thought to be followed by another relatively related thought.* **The function of consciousness** *is to allow sequential thoughts or any other forms of sequential mentation to occur.* Without consciousness, all of the stored information of the cerebral cortex, of the Cerebral-Self, would be unavailable for the process of problem-solving, and without sequential mentation, the next step in the use of consciousness, the Functional-Self would not be adequately effective in solving problems and maintaining the organization of the self.

This defines consciousness and describes its function, but we have not as yet addressed the question of the possible epiphenomenalism of consciousness and its implied infinite regression. To answer the question of infinite regression, a brief review of the concepts presented thus far will be necessary. **The sovereign drive of life** *is the maintenance of its organization.* Increased integration within an organization increases its probability of survival. This increasingly complex integration of the organization, however, must be a functional integration, one in which the complexity does not impede its effectiveness. The human central nervous system with its astronomical number of components has an enormous capacity for integration. The Invested-Self is even more integrated with the limbic system than is the larger store of information that is the Cerebral-Self. But under the goading of disruptive, unfamiliar stimulation and a corresponding increase in attentional activation from the limbic system, the Invested-Self would not be a functionally effective integration. Only with the additional integration of the central nervous system afforded by consciousness does the Invested-Self become a functionally effective self. This is why I've also termed the conscious self the "Functional-Self."

The affective state of the Invested-Self is the degree of familiarity called **belongingness.** While functioning as an Invested-Self, the limbic system activation of an individual is this feeling of heightened familiarity. In other words, as long as the level of integration of the central nervous system called the Invested-Self is capable of handling the patterns of stimulation impinging upon the central nervous system and thereby maintaining the organization of the organism, the affective state or feeling that is occurring is "belongingness." Unfamiliar patterns of stimulation may trigger the affect of excessive "unfamiliarity," which might then trigger arousal, focusing, and consciousness.

But who is experiencing familiarity and unfamiliarity? Is the Invested-Self experiencing familiarity? Is the Functional-Self experiencing consciousness of the Invested-Self? The answer is, *there is no experiencing—there is only experience.* You are not experiencing yourself—you *are* yourself. The Functional-Self is a level of integration of the central nervous system in which an internal representation of the external world, located in the Cerebral-Self, is accompanied by the limbic system excitation of "recognition." At that moment, the synthesis of the feeling of recognition with the internal representation of the self *is* the self. When that moment of recognition, that synthesis, passes and is replaced by a new synthesis, there is a new self. The central nervous system is in a constant state of flux, and the totality of self, which is made up of the many levels of integration of self, is also in a constant state of flux. Therefore, there is no one self that is experiencing the external world and itself—*there is an endless series of selves.*

But there *is* a relative continuity or constancy *of self* that is afforded by the general constancy of the environment and the relative constancy of the vast number of lambda systems or neuron assemblies stored in the Invested-Self. There is a relative constancy of the self afforded by the relative constancy of the feeling of belongingness that is associated with the Invested-Self. Therefore, *the* **constancy of the self** *is the ongoing experience of recognition and familiarity that is associated with the Invested-Self.* This component of the Functional-Self is always the same pattern of activation of the limbic system. In other words, the self, whether the Invested-Self or the Functional-Self, is a phenomenon that occurs at a particular level of integration of the central nervous system. When that level of integration of the central nervous system is not occurring the self exists only as potential. When that level of the central nervous system exists, the self exists, and the experience of self exists. They are all the same. You do not experience your world and yourself— you *are* the experience of your world and yourself.

This explanation of consciousness is of course a variation of the "identity thesis". In essence, it suggests that the phenomenon of our experience of consciousness and the neurophysiological activity of the central nervous system are one and the same. But this thesis, even as explained above, might not be entirely satisfying to lay people. We want to have the feeling of being something more permanent than a moment-to-moment transition from self to self. Therefore, even though the identity thesis, as here described, might avoid the problem of infinite regression, it does not do away with the unacceptable thought that our consciousness and therefore our selves are merely epiphenomenal. Moreover, we want to have the feeling that we are directing our interaction with our world. In other words, we want to have freewill rather than being forced to think of ourselves as will-o-the-wisps of chance.

This desire for greater continuity and control of the self may be a reflection of, and explained by, the principle of increasing integration in the phenomena of life. When the Invested-Self and then the Functional-Self developed from the Cerebral-Self, there was a more effective satisfaction of the sovereign drive for maintenance of the organization of the human organism. These new levels of integration of the central nervous system, with their accompanying feelings of familiarity and recognition, become the new levels of organization of living matter that must be maintained. On the neurophysiological level of conceptualization, this new state of integration of the central nervous system is a complex pattern of neurons that includes internal representations encompassing not just one moment of consciousness but a vast number of moments of consciousness. This super-lambda system is activated when the focus of consciousness shifts from external reality to internal reality, when the focus shifts from concern primarily with the excitation of the external senses to the excitation of one lambda system by another or, in other words, when the focus of consciousness is on sequential mentation rather than on external sensation. On the psychological level of conceptualization, this super-lambda system is the "Self-Concept-Self."

Before we can discuss self-concepts and the Self-Concept-Self, however, and thereby attempt an explanation of our desire for self-control and freewill, it will be necessary to discuss an intervening level of self integration, the Self-Aware-Self.

The Self-Aware-Self

Consciousness is a process that allows sequential mentation to occur. It is also the experience of a specific feeling, the feeling of recognition that accompanies the internal representation that is at the moment being "recognized." The function of consciousness is to temporarily release a greater portion of the informational content of the cerebral cortex from the inhibition necessitated by the attentional and focusing excitation emanating from the limbic system. Unless consciousness or something like it develops within the central nervous system, the organism would continually focus on the source of any unfamiliar pattern of stimulation that impinges upon the central nervous system. Without consciousness, the inhibition of the remainder of the cerebral cortex would make it unlikely that new behavior would be created to cope with the source of stimulation. Consciousness is a level of integration of the central nervous system in which both focusing and free access to the total cerebral cortex is possible. However, until the Invested-Self is differentiated from the Cerebral-Self, consciousness is not possible. In the early ontological development of the human central nervous system, most patterns of stimulation impinging upon the central nervous system are unfamiliar. At the same time, the capacity to focus is also rudimentary. Fortunately, most threatening forms of stimulation are removed by protective parents so that the developing infant does not often have to use consciousness to solve the problem of excessive stimulation. The infant gradually becomes habituated to the consistent external stimulation coming from its relatively restricted world and from its body schema. Through this process, the Invested-Self slowly develops. Once the Invested-Self has developed, and the young organism's capacity to focus has also developed, there will be a store of lambda system generalizations that the unfamiliar incoming stimulation can activate. The relatively simple lambda systems of an infant will already be associated, through habituation, with the limbic system excitation or feeling of "recognition." For example, the infant will recognize the mother's breast, move toward it, and all will soon be well.

As the infant experiences more of its world, more information in stored in its Cerebral-Self. Therefore more potential organization-maintaining lambda systems are available for consciousness to enable differentiation of the self from the not-self so as to further develop the Invested-Self. Then, having more lambda systems that might be relatively similar to the Invested-Self will facilitate the process of consciousness, and consciousness will occur more readily.

Moreover, the Cerebral-Self, having a larger store of information, provides a richer source of potential new combinations of lambda systems, some of which may activate behavior that will be effective in coping with new unfamiliar stimulation, and the Invested-Self will continue to become even more effective. Likewise, the Invested-Self may become more varied as well as more integrated, and also a more pleasurable state, since this ever-increasing number of associations between the Invested-Self and the limbic system feeling of "recognition" might be recognition of events that maintain and enhance the infant's organization.

However, in terms of pain or pleasure, the feeling of recognition is essentially neutral. It is merely a feeling that something is known and a part of past experience. Past experience is not always pleasant, and therefore some of the contents stored in the Cerebral-Self or even in the Invested-Self may be unpleasant and stimulate unpleasant feelings. But most of the time, since consciousness and recognition leads to problem-solutions and reduction of threatening unfamiliar stimulation, recognition will come to have a positive valence. Therefore, the first associated limbic system response to the limbic system feeling of "recognition" is usually a positive feeling. It is this positive feeling that temporarily reduces the anxiety, attention, and focusing, and allows consciousness to proceed. When the new cerebral content that has been facilitated by consciousness fails to result in behavior that copes with the unfamiliar stimulation, then anxiety, attention, and focusing return. In other words, if the end product of the process of consciousness is recognition associated with some inevitably painful cerebral content, then consciousness and recognition would no longer reduce anxiety.

If the organism continues to survive, this association between recognition and inevitable and enduring pain must be the exception rather than the rule. Most of the time, recognition is associated with pleasure and, therefore, consciousness is associated with pleasure. It seems reasonable, therefore, that those increasingly integrated neuronal assemblies that make up the Invested-Self would become the focus of consciousness. When there is no immediate disruptive unfamiliar stimulation impinging upon the central nervous system, and yet the cerebral cortex is generally aroused by the limbic system, the organism that is constantly seeking to maintain its organization through increased integration of its central nervous system will use the process of consciousness to facilitate that increased integration. The pleasure associated with consciousness is, in effect, the state of the organism in the process of increasing its organization through further integration of its components. In other words, when an organism is in the process of increasing the integration of its organization, it is a state of pleasure; and when an organism is in a state of disruption of its organization, or disintegration of its organization, it is in a state of pain.

When the developing organism reaches the level of central nervous system integration in which it is capable of focusing on the Invested-Self and using consciousness to facilitate the further integration of the Invested-Self, it has reached the level of self-development that is termed, the **Self-Aware-Self.** In the early stages of the development of the Self-Aware-Self, the focus of consciousness is probably on bodily pleasures and other physical sensations. The Self-Aware-Self, however, is a more integrated self than the Functional-Self. While the Functional-Self is focusing on solving the problem of the unfamiliar stimulation, the cerebral neuron assemblies that represent various bodily sensations are undoubtedly being activated, but they are not the focus of consciousness. The Self-Aware-Self is using the process of consciousness, or the Functional-Self, to further integrate these bodily sensations into the increasing integration of the central nervous system that is the Invested-Self. From focusing on simple sensations, the Self-Aware-Self may move to focusing on the body's reactions to the environment. This self-study facilitates the refinement of those lambda systems that are predictive models of the reactions of the world to the body's movement. Thus, the Self-Aware-Self facilitates the central nervous system's capacity to predict events in the external world, thereby increasing its probability of maintaining its organization.

Whenever the Self-Aware-Self further integrates aspects of the Invested-Self, it is creating increasingly complex categories of information about the self. When, through focusing on the self, there is recognition that stroking one's leg results in pleasure, there is now an internal representation within the Invested-Self that stores this information. It is recognized that stroking one's side also gives pleasure, and stroking one's arm also gives pleasure. There can now be an internal representation within the Invested-Self that combines all three activities. "If I stroke any place on my body, I will receive pleasure." The chance stroking of any other part of the body may now activate the internal representation of this category of behavior, and the expected experience of the organism would be to experience more pleasure.

This kind of internal representation is a crude categorization within the central nervous system of motor behaviors. Generalizations from this crude categorization are a natural system's property of the organization of the central nervous system. The central nervous system is not capable of making internal representations of every external phenomenon, but these crude categorizations may become more integrated. Neuronal networks that naturally occur within the central nervous system create cell assemblies that are similar enough to the new pattern of incoming stimulation to be activated by that incoming stimulation. When this activated cell assembly further activates efferent neurons and motor behavior, the result caused in the environment by that behavior will further refine the crude internal categorization.

It is a natural system's property of the anatomical and biochemical structure of the central nervous system that it develops categories of internal representations of the world and that it makes generalizations from these categories. *Therefore,* **the Self-Aware-Self,** *in focusing on aspects of the Invested-Self, begins to make categories about the self and generalizations from these categories. These categories are termed,* **self-concepts,** and the compendium of all the most frequently activated self-concepts is the Self-Concept-Self.

The Self-Concept-Self

Because of the nature of the anatomy and the biochemistry of the central nervous system, soon after the development of the Self-Aware-Self, concepts *about* the self are developed. Therefore, as was stated earlier, the Self-Aware-Self is a transitional stage from the Functional-Self to the level of the central nervous system integration that is termed "the Self-Concepts-Self."

The term "self-concept," however, is a misnomer. There are *numerous* self-concepts. We develop self-concepts about most aspects of our Invested-Self. Even though the central nervous system automatically makes categories or generalizations, any specific bit of knowledge about ones Invested-Self does not make a self-concept. For example, I stub my toe, and I focus on that offended member. Since I am familiar with this kind of experience, it is an aspect of my Invested-Self. But I do not have a lambda system in my Invested-Self that would cause me to generalize from this self-awareness that the next time I move my foot I will stub my toe. If the next ten times I move my foot, however, I do stub my toe, I may develop a lambda system that will cause me to predict that whenever I move my foot I will stub my toe. This more integrated lambda system, containing more bits of information, might now be a self-concept, one that could be characterized by the statement, "I am a toe-stubber." Self-concepts develop through experiences, mediated by consciousness and the Self-Aware-Self.

On the neurophysiological level, self-concepts *are complex integrated lambda systems. On* **the psychological level, self-concepts** *are generalizations drawn from individual experiences that synthesize aspects of the Invested-Self.* Based upon these generalizations, predictions can be made about how effective one's behavior might be in situations covered by the generalization.

When viewed from either the neurophysiological or the psychological levels of abstraction, self-concepts are more convenient and potentially more effective ways of processing information. Having stubbed my toe on ten different objects, I would need ten different lambda systems, each of which must be associated with the efferent neuron lambda system that coordinates the motor behavior enabling me to avoid stubbing my toe. Even with all of these lambda systems involved, however, I would have no way of avoiding stubbing my toe in a totally new situation. However, with one self-concept lambda system, "I am a toe-stubber," I would need only one lambda system associated with the neurons system that coordinates the motor behavior, and this one system would protect me against most other toe-stubbing situations perhaps by making me generally more cautious while walking.

Like a simple lambda system, these highly complex and integrated self-concept lambda systems are activated as a unit. The total unit, in turn, may then activate more behavior, or other neuronal units within the cerebral cortex, or feelings from the limbic system. On the psychological level, this also means that self-concepts may have an affective component. When the self-concept, "I am a toe-stubber," is activated, either by an environmental situation or by mentation, the associated limbic system excitation may be experienced as any number of feelings or a combination of feelings. I may feel "ashamed" in realizing that I am a toe-stubber. I may feel "amused," "annoyed," "disgusted," or "sad." On the other hand, it is just as likely that there may be very little activation of my limbic system when I think of myself as a toe-stubber. Perhaps I don't do much walking anyway, so my toe-stubbing self-concept may have little relevance for me. Self-concepts may be essentially descriptive, with little associated affect, or they may be a value, with a considerable loading of affect.

However, it is important to remember that whatever affect is activated by the self-concept will effect the motivation to behave in response to that self-concept. Most lambda systems, including self-concepts, are located in the cerebral cortex, and therefore they coordinate behavior. Feelings, emanating from the limbic system, increase the arousal level and sensitivity of the cerebral cortex and, therefore, feelings act as motivation for behavior. The cerebral cortex and the limbic system always act in unison, or motor behavior and mentation do not occur. The kind and the intensity of the resulting behavior depends upon the pattern of the relationships between the lambda system in the cerebral cortex and the specific locus of activation in the limbic system, or, in other words, between mentation and feeling. Certain self-concepts, therefore, may have profound effects upon behavior. The self-concept, "I am a worthwhile person," may activate feelings of confidence, enthusiasm, and pleasure. The self-concept, "I am a worthless person," may activate feelings of self-disgust, helplessness, and depression.

The Invested-Self is a repository of bits of information that, when activated by an intense enough limbic system response of "familiarity," is differentiated from the larger repository of information that is the Cerebral-Self. Through the medium of consciousness and the Self-Aware-Self, these bits of similar information are further integrated into self-concepts. Although any bit of information in the Invested-Self may activate an associated feeling, and therefore effect behavior, it is likely that more complex and integrated self-concepts will have a greater number of interconnections with the limbic system and efferent neurons and also a higher probability of being similar to and therefore able to activate other lambda systems within the cerebral cortex. For example, I know that needles are sharp and, therefore, I am cautious when using them. This information is a part of my Cerebral-Self. But since I don't often use needles, this information will have relatively little effect upon my behavior. If I am a tailor, needles may be a part of my Invested-Self, but they may still only effect my behavior by making me cautious when using needles. If, however, I realize that I have a phobia about needles then I have a self-concept relative to needles—I am a "needlephobic." This particular self-concept, when activated by the presence of a needle, may now have considerably more effect upon my behavior. More feelings will be aroused, and I may be motivated to retreat from the presence of a needle.

Finally, I may have an even more complex and integrated self-concept associated with needles. I may consider myself to be a master tailor, and stimulated by the sight of a needle, I may feel pride, enthusiasm, aspiration, and inspiration. The needle may initiate thoughts of creative design, fame, and wealth, and I may be motivated to begin an ambitious, artistic, and commercial venture.

Therefore, when an individual reaches the level of self-development represented by the Self-Concepts-Self, through the use of these integrated components of the central nervous system, the individual has the potential for more efficient and effective behavior toward the maintenance of the organization of the organism. Unfortunately, however, self-concepts may be in conflict. On a neurophysiological level, two lambda systems may exist within the same central nervous system that are sensitive to the same pattern of external stimulation, or the same pattern of stimulation from another lambda system. But these two lambda systems may activate two different and incompatible behaviors. The result is a pattern of neurophysiological disorganization that violates the sovereign drive of the organism for maintenance of its organization. On the psychological level, the two self-concepts may be in conflict. For example, "I am a nonviolent person," may exist along with the self-concept, "I must protect my child." When my child is threatened, these two self-concepts are in conflict, and my behavior is not likely to be efficient and effective when my child is threatened. To become more efficient and effective, I need to develop a more integrated central nervous system. I need to develop to the next higher level of self-integration the Integrated-Self.

The Integrated-Self

According to this **theory of self-development,** *given a normal human central nervous system and a supportive social environment, a human being will inevitably develop through six levels of self-integration.* The development of the next two levels, the Integrated-Self and the Transcendent-Self, are not inevitable. In fact, their development may be the exception in human development rather than the rule.

Given a normal central nervous system, even in the uterus the human being has limbic system activation and feelings. Through genetics, the human being is given a vast store of information as the basis for the development of the Cerebral-Self. In the uterus, and through learning, the individual rapidly increases the amount of information stored in the Cerebral-Self. Stability and sameness in the infant's environment, along with the relatively fixed structure of the body and the associated body schema, make it inevitable that some of the information stored in the Cerebral-Self will be more familiar than other information, and therefore the Invested-Self will inevitably develop. The Functional-Self, or consciousness, is a process that occurs naturally because the familiar or known has become associated through learning with the reduction of anxiety, and this reduction of anxiety temporarily reduces the intensity of attention and focusing behavior, thereby enabling mentation to proceed. The human being that survives, survives by further differentiating the Invested-Self from the Cerebral-Self. This process is facilitated by the use of consciousness to focus on the Invested-Self. Given the natural system-property of the central nervous system to create generalizations or concepts, self-concepts inevitably develop through functioning of consciousness and the Self-Aware-Self. The specificity to which individuals articulate self-concepts may vary considerably. A pain-producing environment or a diseased body may considerably reduce the pleasure associated with the experience of consciousness, in general, and more specifically in the Self-Aware-Self. Therefore, less time might be spent in the Self-Aware-Self, thereby reducing the likelihood that clearly articulated self-concepts will develop in such individuals.

The development of the Integrated-Self requires the development of clearly articulated self-concepts. Therefore, the development of the Integrated-Self requires a considerable investment of time in the Self-Aware-Self. This means, of course, that the person who will eventually develop an Integrated-Self must have been very effective in the use of the Functional-Self in solving problems in the earlier stages of development so that consciousness and the Self-Aware-Self will be desirable experiences.

In the Integrated-Self, conflicts between self-concepts have been resolved through the development of higher level, or more abstract, self-concepts, or by ordering the self-concepts according to their degree of relevance to the maintenance of the organization of the organism. These higher level self-concepts and their prioritized value for the individual has been clearly articulated and they are unequivocally associated with affect so that situations or patterns of stimulation from the environment or internal patterns of stimulation from mentation will readily arouse these self-concepts and result in effective and efficient behavior to coordinate and facilitate the maintenance of the organization. Remember, the goal of life is maintaining its organization, and all things an organism does to maintain its organization are sub goals of that primary goal. The **Integrated-Self** *is one that possesses clearly articulated goals and strongly-felt values that are readily available to consciousness.* Moreover, in the Integrated-Self, these goals and values are for the most part *compatible,* not in conflict. These goals and values will clarify ambiguity and make behavior more efficiently goal-directive.

While the less integrated person who holds the incompatible self-concepts of nonviolence and the necessity for defending a child may be inhibited from acting aggressively when the child is threatened by an aggressor, the individual with an Integrated-Self may have already prioritized these two self-concepts. It might have been concluded that the child's well being has a higher value than nonviolence. This more abstract value or higher priority of value would be activated by the threatening situation. Counter aggression would then be swift.

Having clearly articulated and prioritized or non- conflicting values does not make the Integrated-Self an inflexible self. Remember, self-concepts are generalizations, and generalizations are not absolutes. Clearly defined generalizations are activated because the situations that activate them are clearly defined. When these clearly defined generalizations are activated they reduce anxiety and enable consciousness to facilitate mentation or action. If the situation is less clearly defined, these clearly defined generalizations will not be activated. Other less clearly defined lambda systems or generalizations will be activated to begin the search, through consciousness, for creative solutions to the ambiguous situation. Therefore, having an Integrated-Self and clearly articulated self-concepts will not guarantee problem-solving, but it *will* make the process generally more effective and efficient.

For most humans, the Integrated-Self is all that may be achieved, and all that will be necessary to maintain the human organization so that the individual may live a productive and meaningful life. But there is an eight level of self-development that is possible for humans, the Transcendent-Self. Before this level can be fully explained, we must discuss a number of relevant explanatory concepts. The Transcendent-Self will be explained in the chapter on "Transcending the Self."

Now the Self has Purpose

The Function of the Self

The various levels of integration of the self develop because each more highly integrated level is more effective than the previous level in maintaining or enhancing the organization of the organism. Let us summarize and elaborate on why and how the self develops.

The sovereign motivation of organisms is the maintenance of the molecular organization that defines life. This living organization is a dynamic process. In a totally static environment, life would not exist since life is defined as an organization that tends to increase the integration of its organization as a strategy for maintaining its organization, and there would be no purpose for such "growth" in a static environment. Life evolved in a chaotic and ever-changing environment. Life is a moment of organization in an otherwise disorganized universe. It is an entropy in the midst of entropy. Therefore, regarding life as defined the concept of homeostasis is only applicable in a relative sense. An organism that seeks only homeostasis would grow only when goaded by the environment. Life is stimulated to grow first because of *and then in spite of* the environment.

Growth might be may an adding-to, as when the jellyfish adds additional cells to its colony of cells. Or growth may be an increase in integration between cells. It is hypothesized that integration of cells gives a higher probability of survival of the living organization. Therefore, most living forms seek to increase the integration of their organizations. The human organism has evolved to a point where, at birth, it possesses the most integrated cellular structure in the *known* universe. Yet, through maturation and learning, the process of cellular integration within the central nervous system continues rapidly after birth. The motivation for this increased cellular and organizational integration can be conceptualized on neurophysiological and psychological levels of abstraction. In general, on the neurophysiological level, once a level of neuronal integration has been established, if an external or internal stimulation activates the body's sensory neurons, a central nervous system neuron assembly must be activated that resonates with that pattern of incoming stimulation or the cerebral cortex will be in some degree of disorganization. Cerebral cortex disorganization triggers activation of the limbic system, which further affects the cerebral cortex to coordinate attentional and focusing behavior. Then, as has been previously described, through the use of consciousness there is an attempt to integrate the disturbing pattern of stimulation.

The vast majority of incoming patterns of stimulation do not disrupt the organization of the central nervous system because there already exists, in the Cerebral-Self, a lambda system that is similar enough to the incoming pattern of stimulation to be activated and to allow the process of coping with the incoming stimulation to proceed. Activation of attentional and focusing behavior is not always necessary, and it would occur less frequently if the human organism was primarily motivated to maintain homeostasis. But since the human organism is motivated to increase its integration, the process of consciousness, once established, will be engaged more and more frequently, even when there is no external source of disruptive stimulation. Once the human organism is biochemical aroused, or awake, mentation is a regular activity because mentation is one of the human organism's primary ways of enhancing its integration.

In discussing mentation and higher levels of integration of the central nervous system, it is convenient to conceptualize the motivational process in psychological rather than in neurophysiological terms. It is hoped that it is now evident how these psychological terms have been extrapolated logically from the neurological level of conceptualization. In using these psychological terms, we are not talking about a different kind of phenomena, merely a more complex level of integration of the same phenomena. Human life, like one-cell life, is still a pattern of cellular organization, and the maintenance and enhancement of this organization, through increased integration of the organization, is the sovereign motivation of human life as it is in single-cell life. The major difference between the more complex integrations of life and simple integrations of life are the methods used to maintain and enhance the living organization.

The primary psychological terms I will be using will be various kinds of feelings, forms of mentation, and the various levels of self-integration previously described. The presence of a feeling means that there has been activation of some loci in the limbic system. But all activation of the limbic system is not necessarily some form of feeling. Feelings only occur through the mediation of consciousness. In other words, *there must be some degree of recognition, however vague, that a feeling is occurring for the term "feeling" to be applied to the phenomenon.* The recognition may be no more than a vague awareness that something is affecting the self, but that vague awareness is, nevertheless, an indication of a synthesis between an activation in the limbic system and an activation in the cerebral cortex.

Feelings are Motivators

The two general categories of motivational feelings are pleasant and unpleasant feelings. The simplest motivational synthesis between the limbic system and the cerebral cortex exists when an unpleasant feeling is occurring and there is consciousness, or "recognition," that something unpleasant is happening. The Functional-Self or the Self-Aware-Self may enable the individual to further define that unpleasant something. There are apparently specific locations within the limbic system for any pleasant or unpleasant feeling that we can define. Henceforth, I will usually refer to feelings when describing the functioning of the self. But always be aware that these feelings are indications, at the psychological level of abstraction, that there is an underlying neurophysiological event occurring.

Unpleasant feelings are feelings such as anxiety, pain, depression, frustration, annoyance, disgust, nausea, fear, anger, rage, hatred, inadequacy, helplessness, hopelessness, despair, or weakness. The unpleasant feelings motivate the individual to seek causes of these unpleasant feelings. With unpleasant feeling, there is disruption or disintegration in the pattern of organization at the neurophysiological level of the central nervous system. Innate or reflexive motor patterns and learned motor patterns have been established to attack, to change, or to flee from the source triggering these unpleasant feelings. The human organism is motivated to reduce these unpleasant feelings so as to return to a relative state of homeostasis or to the previous level of central nervous system organization and integration.

Pleasant feelings are obviously different from unpleasant feelings, but the difference is even more than it seems. Pleasant feelings are feelings such as joy, rapture, anticipation, excitement, love, affection, appreciation, respect, pride, contentment, hope, serenity, or various forms of ecstatic experiences. Some of these feelings may be indications of a degree of homeostasis within the central nervous system. Serenity may be pleasurable because the central nervous system is at a steady-state of organization and integration. But serenity is most desirable when the organism is in a state of disruption, when one is feeling unpleasant feelings. On the other hand, after long periods of homeostasis, serenity may get boring. Therefore, most of the pleasant feelings are not desirable because of their homeostatic quality. Many or perhaps most pleasant feelings are desirable because they are occurring when the central nervous system is in a dynamic rather than in a homeostatic state. These pleasant feelings are associated with change, with an increase from one level of integration of the central nervous system to a higher level, or in anticipation of such a positive change. These pleasant feelings are usually associated with the recognition or consciousness that something positive is occurring, or is about to occur, or might occur. Therefore, the human organism may at times seek homeostasis, but just as often and perhaps more often, it seeks the temporary disruption in homeostasis that is associated with change in the central nervous system from one level of integration to a higher level of integration.

An example of such growth-related pleasure-seeking is the anticipation of enjoyment on a vacation. A vacation is a change in environment, a change from the familiar to an unfamiliar and therefore a disorganizing stimulation. Yet, we eagerly seek vacations. We are not seeking disruption and disorganization, we are seeking new experiences that will enrich our Cerebral-Selves and perhaps even be incorporated into our Invested-Selves so that we can be, in becoming familiar with these new environments, more integrated beings. We seek this increased integration of the central nervous system, and of ourselves, and we seek the feelings associated with this seeking, the pleasurable feelings of anticipation, excitement, curiosity, admiration, or understanding.

This growth-associated pleasure-seeking should not be confused with the excessive pleasure-seeking that might result from an overload of unpleasant feelings. When one is in pain, depressed, or otherwise experiencing unpleasant feelings, one may seek to ameliorate these feelings by blotting out the pain through compulsive involvement in activities that have in the past produced pleasure, activities such as compulsive sex or eating. The desire, in this case, is not further integration of the central nervous system. This is an example of one of the complex psychological coping mechanisms that our complicated and highly integrated central nervous systems have developed. Just as consciousness results in the temporary reduction of anxiety, through activation of the incompatible feeling of recognition, so we have learned to focus mentation away from disruptive stimulation or mentation onto those forms of mentation that are associated with pleasurable feelings. In this fashion, we temporarily obviate the disruptive stimulation and its associated unpleasant feeling. Such mechanisms are frequently necessary in coping with periods of excessive disruptive stimulation, but they sometimes become habitual and, in the long run, ineffective as methods for maintaining and enhancing the organization of the human organism. The psychological coping mechanisms will be described and explained in more detail later.

Mentation is its Own Purpose

On the neurophysiological level, mentation occurs when there is activation of a lambda system in the cerebral cortex that has previously been established as an internal representation of the external or internal world. These lambda systems may also be activated without the occurrence of mentation. This occurs when the lambda systems have been previously associated, through learning, with efferent neuron systems that coordinate habitual behavior. Mentation only occurs when, through consciousness, the feeling of "recognition" is needed to temporarily reduces the anxiety that is associated with the failure of that lambda system to automatically activate an activity to reduce the necessity for the focusing behavior. As previously indicated, this temporary reduction of anxiety reduces the focusing behavior and disinhibits a larger area of the cerebral cortex, making available other lambda systems for possible activation. **Mentation** *is a process; it is the sequential activation, through the medium of consciousness, of one lambda-system-internal-representation by another lambda-system-internal-representation.*

There are many forms of mentation. The simplest kind of mentation may be the continuous firing of very similar lambda-systems, as in a sensation. When we become aware of a sensation, it means that nerve endings are being stimulated in some area of the body, and there has been neural activation in the parietal lobes of the cerebral cortex. At times we may have mentation related to a simple sensation, as when we concentrated on an on-going pain, but most such stimulation, being of low intensity, does not reach our awareness, which is to say, there is no corresponding activation of the limbic system feeling of "recognition." In other words, there is no consciousness of the sensation. Sensations are probably contained in relatively simple cell assemblies, and the continuation of the sensation is usually based upon a continuation of the peripheral stimulation of the nerve endings.

We may also have mentation related to a sensation that is not currently being stimulated. This happens when we remember how we felt when we were experiencing a sensation. This vicarious experience is seldom as intense as the original sensation. For example, try to remember, right now, how it felt to have a toothache. About all you can feel is a vague awareness of your teeth. Memory of a sensation is mentation consisting of the activation of the limbic system feeling of "recognition" and the activation of a cerebral cortex cell assembly representing the mentation associated with that sensation, perhaps a words that depicts the sensation such as the word, pain. On the other hand, when you are actually experiencing a toothache, you are conscious of the pain and where in your mouth you are feeling the pain. Therefore, there is a reverberation between the peripheral nerve, the parietal lobes, the lambda system within the cerebral cortex representing the words describing the quality of the sensation, the location of the source of the sensation, and the feeling of "recognition" in the limbic system. When a toothache is alleviated there is only the memory of that sensation, consisting of the word-representational-lambda-system (pain) and the limbic system "recognition." Therefore, the memory of a sensation pales in comparison to the actual sensation.

We must remember to differentiate sensations from feelings. **Sensations** *are peripheral activations of nerve endings that in turn activate areas of the parietal lobes.* **Feelings** *are activations of the limbic system that are differentiated from other activations of the limbic system in* *that feelings, through the medium of consciousness, are in synthesis with some area of the cerebral cortex.* When we are experiencing sensations, we may also be experiencing feelings related to our sensations. But they are two different experiences. Feelings may activate mentation, and mentation may activate feelings, and one neurophysiological process never occurs without the other. But they are neurophysiologically discrete excitations, and it is their relationship, one to the other, that accounts for the quality of the experience. You may have a memory of a past anxiety attack in which, as you calmly review the past experience, there is considerable excitation of the cerebral cortex. Since you are now calm, there will be relatively little excitation of the limbic system associated with that review. Or you may recall that anxiety attack so vividly that you are overwhelmed by activation of the limbic system feeling of anxiety, and you are even unable to think clearly enough to remember any of the details of the experience. In this case there is a relatively greater activation within the limbic system than in the cerebral cortex. Therefore, there may be mentation related to feelings, but feelings are primarily a limbic system phenomenon, and mentation is primarily a cerebral cortex phenomenon.

Mentation associated with lambda-systems located in other areas of the cortex may be more vividly and directly experienced within the cerebral cortex. Auditory mentation is represented in the temporal lobes, and visual mentation is represented in the occipital lobes. We are able to recall songs and imagine scenes with enough detail and intensity to evoke strong feelings. In dreams, and even at times when we are awake, we may even be convinced that these internal representations are immediate representations of external reality. In other words, we may hallucinate.

But the activation of a cerebral cortex cell assembly that makes possible the internal representation of external reality is only a model of the external world; it is not an exact replica. Even mentation that is being directly activated by peripheral stimulation is not an exact recording of what is occurring in the external world. The peripheral nerves are not sensitive to all kinds and across the full range of any kind of energy. Moreover, the lambda systems within the cerebral cortex have evolved to respond to a range of patterns of energy not to all possible patterns. In other words, there is not one lambda system for every possible pattern of stimulation. Therefore, what we immediately experience of the external world is an approximation, and approximation that we are usually refining as we continue to receive external input about the external world.

Mentational Effectiveness and Efficiency Mentation that is activated from within the cerebral cortex as one lambda system activates another, as in memory or imagination, is an even less detailed representation of external reality. Memory and imagination are cut off from the continual refining process afforded by immediate and continued stimulation from the external world. This is both a plus and a minus. Memory and imagination are not as accurate as immediate perception of the external world, but this relative freedom from detail makes it possible for one lambda system to activate a relatively dissimilar lambda system and therefore to rapidly create many new combinations of experiences. The increased speed of mentation over perception presents many more possible solutions to problems through mentation than would occur if mentation were precisely correlated with external reality.

Language: Our Most Efficient Mentation

Simplicity or reduced detail and speed of interactive activation may be one reason why language is our most effective form of mentation. Speech and language usage is represented in the frontal/temporal lobes in interaction with the frontal lobes. Just as sight and hearing are only abstractions of the information from the external world, words are even more abstracted representations of experience. To **abstract** *is to pull from the whole substance an essence of the substance.* The essence is then used to represent the whole. My occipital representation of the actually sight of my mother captures enough of the details of that person to evoke recognition and feelings other than mere recognition. The spoken name "Mother" is a far less complex pattern of external stimulation, and yet it also evokes recognition and feelings, and sometimes very powerful feelings. The occipital representation is an abstraction of the actual information in the external world, and the name "Mother" is a further abstraction of that external reality. The cell assembly required to represent the name "Mother" is probably considerably smaller than the cell assembly required to represent the visual image of my mother. The smaller cell assemblies associated with words make possible a greater storage of word representations as well as the closer proximity of such cell-assemblies. Therefore, rapid intra-activation of the cell assemblies and more complex configurations of the cell assemblies is possible. Moreover, the combination of these abstracted cell assemblies (words) into concepts, principles, theories, and even a book full of theories, such the one you are reading, is facilitated.

Even through words, as abstractions, may be simplified, their very simplification makes possible more complex integration of the central nervous system and of the organization of the human organism. Word usage therefore is a significant advancement in the human organism's pursuit of integration as a means of enhancing the maintenance of its living organization.

The speed of interaction and the creative potential of the numerous combinations that are possible with words makes language usage more efficient for creative problem-solving. Words, on the other hand, being far removed from reality, are capable of considerably distorting reality. Therefore, words are one of the primary components of psychological coping mechanisms, ways that we have developed to distort and deny reality so as to delay the effects of disorganizing stimulation.

For the most part, however, verbal mentation is used effectively to cope with reality. Therefore, verbal mentation comes to be associated with pleasurable affect. When not talking to other people, or listening to other people, or reading other people's words, we do a lot of talking to ourselves. Most of our conscious moments, that is moments of "recognition" or moments of synthesis between the limbic system feeling of "recognition" and cerebral cortex cell assemblies, are moments of consciousness of words. Sometimes we mentate, or think, in non-verbal sounds or in pictures, but usually we think in words. For the typical normal person the predominant method of processing reality is word-processing. Words are so effective that, once we have mastered them, we are highly motivated to use them. Therefore, our selves, our Functional-Selves, and our Self-Aware-selves are primarily verbal selves. Our Integrated-Selves are integrated words or concepts. One of my most familiar self-concepts is a word. When you call my name, I conveniently recognize and differentiate myself from all other selves.

And the Self Has Needs

The Self as Instrument of the Self-as-Goal: A New Variation on an Old Theory of Needs.

The self, and all of its levels, evolved phylogenetically, and it develops ontogenetically *as an instrument* to facilitate the maintenance and enhancement of the organization of individual organisms. But the self of individual organisms eventually becomes its own reason for being. Human beings have even been known to sacrifice their total cellular organizations, or lives, in service of a particular self-concept, the self as father, for example. This valuing of self above life seems to be a contradiction of the assumption that the sovereign motive of organizations is maintenance of organization. We need a theory that will adequately describe and explain this apparent contradiction.

Abraham Maslow's (1954) concept of a hierarchy of needs does a good job of describing this phenomenon, but an explanation of "why" is lacking. Nevertheless, Maslow's hierarchy is a good starting point. I will combine Maslow's theory with the general theory of self thus far described and outline a new theory of needs, one that admittedly is only a variation of Maslow's theory. This theory of needs traces the transition of the self from an instrument to a goal.

Maslow's theory of motivation is primarily a descriptive theory of the variety of needs. **Needs** *are substances or experiences without which the organism would fail to survive or develop.* Maslow described and categorized the various needs that seem to underlie human behavior. He suggested that there are five basic categories of needs. These are the Physiological Needs, the Safety Needs, the Love and Belonging Needs, the Esteem Needs, and the Self-Actualization Need. The Physiological Needs are the most basic. Human beings begin life with the capacity or skills to satisfy some of the Physiological Needs, and most of infancy is spent developing and refining these Physiological Need-satisfying skills. Physiological need-satisfying dominates infancy. Physiological Needs are needs for such substances or experiences as air, water, food, elimination, expiration, and temperature regulation.

Eventually, however, most infants effectively master the physiological need-satisfying skills, and then are freer to begin mastery of the skills required to satisfy another category of needs—the Safety Needs. The Safety Needs are ways of avoiding or mastering any external threat to the existence of the organism. These needs, such as the need to avoid dangerous situations or the need to avoid extremes in weather, exist from the beginning of the infant's life. Maslow suggested that there is an innate inclination to master these Safety Needs but that this mastery cannot begin in earnest until the infant has first mastered the Physiological Needs. Fortunately, the infant's parents usually take care of most of these needs for infants during this period when the infants are ineffective in caring for themselves. *The necessity of a lower-order need to be mastered before the next order need can be satisfied is described as the* **hierarchy of needs**. Then, after the infant has become relatively effective in mastering the Safety Needs, more effort is expended in mastering the Love and Belonging Needs, then the Esteem Needs, and eventually the Self-Actualization Need. Maslow also suggested that, once a higher-level need has become the dominant focus of an individual, that individual might be inclined to deny, at least temporarily, the urgings of the lower-order needs. This was Maslow's explanation for why people might even sacrifice their own lives or, in other words, deny their Safety Needs, in order to defend their loved-one.

Reversing the order of importance of needs is the exception rather than the rule, however. Although mastery of a lower-order need frees a person to invest more effort in satisfaction of the next higher-order need, if there is too much deprivation of the lower-order need, the person will become reinvested in the satisfaction of that lower-order need.

Maslow's Physiological and Safety needs are best explained on the physiological level of conceptualization, but in previous need theories there has been little attempt to explain the transition from biochemical motives to psychological motives as the individual shifts emphasis from the Safety Needs to the Love and Belonging Needs, the Esteem Needs, and the Self-Actualization Need. The theory of needs presented here will attempt to explain this transition, as well as to make adjustments in the need levels that will better describe the way people actually function, all of which will make the theory more internally consistent.

A New Needs Theory

A needs theory is a psychological theory. Specifically, a needs theory is a theory of motivation. The organism is motivated to seek needed substances or experiences. The substances or experiences that are required by the organism are complex substances or complex experiences, and the activity of the organism in seeking and processing these substances or experiences are highly organized activities. Another psychological theory of motivation is the drive theory. Drive theory is concerned with a less complex level of theoretical conceptualization, and it is generally more closely related to the physiological level of conceptualization. Drive theory is also concerned with very general motives, such as the drives to reduce pain or to increase pleasure. At an even lower level of motivational conceptualization is the description of the neurophysiological and biochemical processes that occur when a drive is operating. It must be emphasized that, although one level of theoretical conceptualization may be described as more basic than another, this is not to say that one level of conceptualization is more important than another. Both biological and psychological theories are intended to describe and explain behavior so that it may eventually be possible to predict behavior. The complexity of the level of behavior to be predicted governs which level of conceptualization theory is most convenient and effective for describing the components that enter into the formula for predicting the behavior. In predicting whether Tom will love Mary rather than Helen, it is more convenient and effective to describe Tom's relationship to his mother than to describe the relationship of his hormonal level to the physiognomy of his gonads.

Nevertheless, the most effective theory of human motivation, at whatever level of conceptualization, must not have hypotheses at one level of conceptualization that do violence to hypotheses that have been reasonably well established at another level of conceptualization. When Tom eventually makes his choice, his hormones and his gonads will undoubtedly play their parts.

Motivational theory is concerned with what pushes and pulls the organism to do something. A *general* theory of motivation, such as the one presented here, must apply to all levels of theoretical conceptualization. This motive must function at the biochemical level, at the cellular level, at the level of systems of cells, and at the psychological levels of drives, basic needs, and self-concepts. A needs theory is a type of motivational theory that focuses on the specific substances or events that do the pushing or pulling. Maslow's needs theory categories and describes the relationship between categories of needs. The substances or events can be relatively simple, as in the need for calcium, or complex, as in the need for love. The emphasis in the present discussion is on the level of complexity of Maslow-like basic needs and on the levels of self-integration. But first it would be worthwhile to describe a motivation theory that is usually concerned with a lower level of need-complexity—drive theory—and to relate need and self-theory to drive theory. **Drives** *describe the interaction between the biochemistry of the blood, the neurophysiology of the central* *nervous system, and motor behavior.* The hunger drive, for instance, is to a certain extent related to the level of glucose in the blood. As the blood flows through the hypothalamus, low levels of blood sugar register in the hypothalamus. This activates hypothalamic neurons, that in turn activate neurons in the hippocampus and the amygdala, that in turn activate cell assemblies in the cerebral cortex, resulting in thoughts of food and motor behavior in pursuit of food. The neurons or neuron assemblies within the limbic system are known as the drive-centers. Apparently, there are drive-centers, or cell assemblies, within the limbic system that, when directly stimulated with electrical probes, result in motor behavior and ideation related to such drives as hunger, avoidance of pain, or sexual desire. This electrical stimulation of the drives centers, however, is not equivalent to the more complex experience of the need-deprivation. *The neurons or neuron assemblies in the drive-centers are just one component in a far more integrated system, and the activation of that one component results in what might be described as* **a simulation of the experience.** People who are subjected to these electrical stimulations of the brain report that the experience is "happening to them" rather than something that is a part of them. This is good example of why the complexity of the behavior to be predicted must be matched with the complexity of the concepts in the prediction formula. To attempt to explain the desire for sirloin steak solely on the basis of one's level of blood sugar or on the activation of a drive-center does not do justice to the integrational complexity of that rich gustatory and culinary experience.

Nevertheless, biochemistry and drive-centers are operating when need-deprivations are operating. Furthermore, at the lower-level needs, drives and biochemistry play a relatively greater part than at the higher level of needs. In other words, at the lower need levels, there are not as many components to be integrated, and relatively more of these components are biological rather than psychological. At these lower levels, behavior will be activated without stimulation from outside of the body. The infant will be hungry whether or not there is a bottle to stimulate that hunger. Therefore, it can be said that the lower level survival needs are more *internally* motivated than the next higher level of needs. But, as it turns out, the highest level of needs once again becomes internally motivated. This will be explained later.

The idea of internally and externally motivation will be incorporated into this new needs theory. The first four levels of needs are as follows:

1. The Internally Motivated Survival Needs,
2. The Externally Motivate Survival Needs,
3. The Externally Satisfied Self-Enhancement Needs,
4. The Internally Satisfied Self-Enhancement Needs.

There is a fifth level of need, The Need for Self-Transcendence, that will also be discussed later.

The **Internally Motivated Survival Needs** *are the same as Maslow's Physiological Needs, that is, the need for air, water, food, etc.* The motive power behind these needs is a change in biochemistry, which in turn affects the drive-centers. Internally Motivated Survival Needs are genetically engineered into the organism. In human beings, these are very complex needs that, phylogenetically, have evolved into marvelously integrated systems for the maintenance of the organism's organization. This genetically triggered and coordinated growth process requires energy and the material for growth. These energy and growth producing materials come from sources external to the organism, but in the Internally Motivated Survival Needs the urge to seek those external materials is always internal. As long as there is a readily available and convenient source of these external substances, and therefore the absence of internal need-deprivation, the Internally Motivated Survival Needs motivate no further interest in the external world.

The *Externally Motivated Survival Needs, however, are triggered by events in the external world. When loud noises occur, when shifts in the environment disrupt the equilibrium of the organism, when noxious chemicals, or excessive weights, or sharp objects impinge upon the organism, the organism responds to protect its organization.* The mechanisms for satisfying these Externally Motivated Survival Needs are more complex and integrated than the mechanisms required for the satisfaction of most of the Internally Motivated Survival Needs. The Externally Motivated Survival Needs require external sense modalities and elaborate integration of reflexive and learned motor behaviors, coupled with the coordinating cell assemblies of the cerebral cortex and the tension arousal and activation components of the limbic system. Much more of the body is involved and there is much more integration in the components of the body when an infant is attempting to defend itself against a taunting sibling than when that same infant is satisfying its hunger needs at its mother's breast.

The Instrument Becomes the Goal: How the Self-Enhancement Needs Evolved

The Internally and the Externally Motivated Survival Needs function effectively to motivate primitive organisms to develop mechanisms that will increase the likelihood of the maintenance of their organizations. Human beings, because of the evolution of their more complex and integrated central nervous systems, begin very early to development even more effective mechanisms to aid in the maintenance and enhancement of organization. Once human children begin to develop their "selves," the association between the complex cell assemblies in the Invested-Self and the pleasurable feelings in the limbic system begin to make this state of integration of the human organism a state that may be as pleasurable as the simpler and more basic organizational states associated with satisfaction of the lower-order needs. Moreover, once the self-states (or processes) have been learned, they are more readily achievable than those states of satisfaction that are dependent upon external substances or events in the environment. Therefore, once these levels of organizational integration have been learned, they may no longer be merely mechanisms for maintenance of the organization. *They may now become goals or motives of the human organism.*

Whether the self-states or processes become goals depends on experience. The pleasurable feelings that are associated with the Invested-Self, the Functional-Self, the Self-Aware-Self, and the Self-Concepts-Self are acquired through experience. In the early development of the human being, and of the self, most of the events that affect the self, either positively or negatively, are beyond the control of the self. Whether the environment treats one kindly is to a large degree governed by one's parents. Conscientious, concerned, and affectionate parents provide those kinds of environmental events that will be experienced by the infant as pleasurable. The pleasurable events will become the familiar events for the infant, and the Invested-Self will become primarily a pleasurable self. The moments of recognition, or consciousness, will also be associated with pleasurable feelings activated in the limbic system, and consciousness will be for the most part a pleasurable experience. Therefore, consciousness of the pleasurable Invested-Self will usually be a pleasurable experience. It is also likely that the self-concepts will be pleasurable, since they are merely abstractions of all of these pleasurable experiences.

On the other hand, parents who do not provide pleasurable environmental events for their children make it likely that all levels of integration of the selves of their children will be unpleasant. Therefore, it is obvious that the developing human being, and the developing self of human beings, is dependent upon external events to shape the nature of the developing self. Since human organisms seek the feelings associated with increased integration rather than with disintegration of its organization, the developing organism will generally seek environmental events that create pleasure and, therefore, integration of the self.

Just as the infant operating on survival level needs will develop skills for satisfying those needs, so the infant will develop skills for enhancing the self through external sources of self-enhancement. This means that a major developmental task for the child is learning to relate effectively to the parents and other human being who provide those pleasurable environmental events.

The *Externally* Satisfied Self-Enhancement Needs *provide the motivation for effectively relating to others.* These needs are similar to Maslow's Love and Belonging Needs. There is a difference, however. Maslow described two levels of Love and Belonging Needs. In the first level, the individual seeks gratification of the Love and Belonging Needs through being loved by others and by being accepted and a part of something. At the second level of the Love and Belonging Needs, this need is satisfied by giving love and by allowing others to be a part of one's self. This second level of Maslow's hierarchy of needs seems to require a much more integrated self and, in my opinion, is more appropriately placed in a higher category of needs. The same misplacement occurs in Maslow's next level of needs, the Esteem Needs. There are two levels of the Esteem Needs. At the first level, people seek esteem through the good opinions of others, and at the second level people seek esteem though having good opinions of themselves. This second level of the Esteem Needs also requires a more integrated self. Therefore, I would prefer to categorize the first level of Maslow's Love and Belonging Needs as the need for self-enhancement through *external* sources and the second levels of Maslow's Love and Belonging Needs *and* his Esteem Needs as the need to enhance one's self through *internal* sources.

In The *Internally* Satisfied Self-Enhancement Needs, the individual must first develop self-concepts that are strongly associated with pleasurable limbic system feelings so that one is motivated to behave in those ways that are consistent with those self-concepts, thereby, activating the pleasurable feelings associated with those self-concepts. Any behavior that is inconsistent with those self-concepts will be experienced as disruptive or disintegrative to the highly integrated state of the central nervous system that is the self-concepts. Therefore, behavior that is inconsistent with these strongly held self-concepts will be avoided. Behavior and events in the external world are involved in the gratification of this level of needs, but it is the existence of the highly integrated state of the central nervous system, which is the Self-Concepts-Self that is the source of that gratification. The person operating on this level of needs may have developed self-concepts that say, "I should love others," or "I should be true to my principles," and therefore it is through behavior that is consistent with such self-concepts that this internal source of pleasure is activated.

Maslow's fifth basic need, **self-actualization,** *is the need to become whatever one has the potential for becoming.* Rather than being a different need, the activities associated with self-actualization seem to be different kinds of strategies for enhancing the self. The concept of what one should become is based upon knowledge of one's self. Therefore, these self-actualization activities belong in the category of the need for self-enhancement from an internal source.

Understanding the Hierarchical Nature of Needs

When an individual has mastered the skills for satisfying one category of basic needs, the individual begins to emphasize satisfaction of the next higher-level category of needs. This was the observation that Maslow made about the way human beings function. He built this observation into his theory of "hierarchical" needs. But why should one category of needs have priority over another, and why should the higher-order needs, which are not required to maintain life, emerge at all?

It is assumed that the human organism is motivated by the sovereign need to maintain its organization by developing greater integration of its organization. This would account for the *order* of the hierarchical needs in this new needs theory, which are arranged in order of increasing integration of the central nervous system.

The four categories of needs are also arranged in order of urgency of need. When an *internal* survival need is aroused, it is because there already exists a disruption in the organization of the organism, whereas, there is a time delay before the survival need that is triggered by an *external* source can have its effect upon the organization of the organism. The complex organization that is the self can exist only if the relatively less complex organization of the physical body is intact. Therefore, because of this necessary chronological sequencing there is greater urgency for satisfaction of the lower-order, physical survival needs than there is for the higher-order self-enhancement needs.

Likewise, there is greater urgency for satisfaction of the self-enhancement needs from an external source than for satisfaction of the self-enhancement needs from an internal source. In the early stages of self-development, the Invested-Self has relatively fewer associations between knowledge of the self and positive limbic system feelings. The undeveloped self is dependent upon pleasure-provoking external experiences, such as praise from a parent, to establish those associations so that the self may achieve an increasing state of integration. Therefore, there may be a delay between the time at which the self is put into a state of disorganization by some negative external experience and the time when the individual can encounter a positive self-enhancing external experience, such as the praise. This delay creates a sense of urgency. When the individual is at the level of self-development in which there are numerous established associations between self-knowledge and positive limbic system feelings, the individual can almost immediately provide his or her own self-affirmation, as when the self has been placed in a state of disequilibria by some disaffirming experience and then reassures his or herself by recalling past successes or the praise he received from his parent for these successes.

Meaningfulness and Meaninglessness

Mastery of the skills for satisfying a category of basic needs may be, in itself, a factor causing the emergence of the next higher-order category of basic needs. To explain this, it is first necessary to describe the concept of "meaningfulness." *An experience is* **meaningful** *if it is cognitively associated with the satisfaction of a need and if it provokes a feeling that to some degree offsets the displeasure associated with the unmet need.* There is usually some delay between the experience of a need-deprivation and the satisfaction of that need. Yet the experience of a need-deprivation is the experience of some degree of disorganization in the organism. Disorganization in the organism is anxiety provoking. Anxiety, if allowed to continue, is a further disorganization of the organism. Human beings have developed an immediate way to at least temporarily control anxiety. Basically, this control consists of generating feelings in the limbic system that are incompatible with anxiety. Mentation is meaningful if it logically relates to the eventual satisfaction of a need. Planning a tasty meal when one is hungry is meaningful mentation. Such mentation is associated with the limbic system feeling of expectation or hope of eventual satisfaction of the need. This limbic system feeling of hope is then incompatible with, and to some degree controls, the anxiety caused by the necessary delay in the gratification of the need.

Moments of need-gratification, however, are relatively infrequent. Far more of one's time is spent in activities or mentations that *eventually* lead to moments of need-gratification. Yet all of that preparation can be pleasurable if it is "meaningful" preparation. For example, eating gratifies the need for food. As has been said, planning a meal and preparing the food is meaningful and can also be pleasurable. Likewise, although growing food is far removed from the actual satisfaction of the need for food, growing food can also be a meaningful and pleasurable activity.

The opposite of meaningful is "meaningless." *Activities or mentations that are unrelated to any need may be cognitively meaningless and experienced as a feeling of* **meaninglessness** *or a feeling of emptiness.* You will recall that the living organization is a dynamic organization. It is constantly modifying its organization to more effectively cope with the ever-changing environment. Activity or mentation in pursuit of the goal of increased integration of the organism is dynamic organization. The human organism is relatively less dynamic in the state of sleep, but it is not in stasis. But when the central nervous system is in a state of limbic system arousal and yet involved in meaningless activity, the natural dynamism of the human organism *is* in stasis. In that state, activity that is not in the pursuit of such a goal has no point around which to organize and is therefore, by its very nature, disorganizing. It follows that meaningless activity eventually becomes anxiety provoking.

Meaningless activity or mentation may result from unclear goals, temporary absence of effective strategies for approaching goals, or, paradoxically, from having achieved goals and gratified needs. When the individual is relatively unskilled at meeting needs, a great deal of time is required to satisfy needs. This time spent in using inefficient skills may be frustrating and to some degree anxiety provoking, but it is nevertheless meaningful activity. On the other hand, the individual who has become very efficient in the use of skills for satisfying needs no longer has to spend much time in using those skills. Needs are satisfied quickly, but then there is also empty time and potential meaninglessness.

It is the occurrence of the feeling of meaninglessness, following the mastery of the skills for gratifying one level of needs that goads the individual into seeking a higher level of self-integration. As was indicated earlier, an increase in the level of self-integration is correlated with the higher hierarchical ordering of the basic needs. When the individual has achieved relative mastery of the skills for satisfying Internally Motivated Survival Needs, the individual is motivated to further integrate the self, and to avoid meaninglessness, and therefore spends more time mastering the skills for satisfying the need for survival from an external source. Having the skill for gratifying these needs, the next level of need becomes a more potent motivator for that individual. If there have been no impediments to the natural order of growth or to the increasing integration of the individual, the individual eventually masters the skills for gratifying the need for self-enhancement from an internal source. Now, is that the end of the process of integration? Is the person "self-actualized," in Maslow's terms? No, if the argument presented thus far is to be followed to its logical conclusion, after mastering the skills for satisfying the highest-order needs, the individual is once again thrown into a state of meaninglessness. Now the self is in a state of integration and yet in a potential state of disintegration because of increasing time spend in the state of meaninglessness. The solution to this dilemma lies in transcending the self.

Consciousness Enables Freewill and Responsibility

Consciousness of What by Whom

Before we address the question of transcending the self, there are still some unresolved, related issues to be considered. Before we go beyond the self, let us try to feel relatively comfortable in our belief that we in fact have a self to go beyond. I have described consciousness or the Functional-Self as a synthesis between a specific mentation and at least the general feeling of recognition, but now I am emphasizing that recognition is usually accompanied by one or more specific feelings. For example, when I *think* I am hungry, I also *recognized* that I *feel* an *emptiness* in my stomach and a general *weakness*. But, in so defining consciousness we may have given consciousness a useful theoretical definition, but we may also have left ourselves with another empty feeling. The above definition describes a process. So we have defined consciousness as a process but failed to clarify who or what is experiencing that process. In everyday experience, we have become accustomed to the notion that *we* not only recognize our thoughts but *we* are also conscious of what *we* are thinking and feeling. It is disconcerting to be told that this process of thinking and feeling *is* us, and we are perhaps no more than a process.

Consciousness and the Self in Historical Perspective

Obviously, understanding consciousness is an age-old challenge. The problem of consciousness is associated with and perhaps the same as what has been called he the mind-body problem and more recently, the mind-brain problem. Rene Descartes (1998) in the 17th century, wanting to feel comfortable that he existed, stated, "I think; therefore, I am." He was also concerned with other issues, such as differentiating the physical body from the mind and clarifying God's part in all of this, but let's not complicated the problem with these venerable issues.

Let's assume that this "I am" that Descartes wanted to prove existed is the same as the self you and I want to be sure exists. Descartes argued that his self must exist because something existed to think about that self. Unfortunately, others have argued that Descartes was guilty of circular reasoning, and they even labeled this the Cartesian circle.

Others have argued that the mind-body problem is created by confused semantics, and in so arguing they have followed Descartes' lead in focusing on thinking as the necessary process for establishing the existence of something other than the physical self. I'm sure that the ambiguity built into our language contributes to our confusion, but in my opinion, it is the emphasis on thinking almost to the exclusion of feeling that is the root of the problem. I will argue that I know that I exist not just because I think but also because I feel. Moreover, my wonderful certainty that I *do* exist is a feeling that only requires that I think about it when another feeling, doubt, rears up to force me to think. At that moment, consciousness, or the synthesis of thoughts and feelings, synthesizes all my Self-Concept-Self lambda systems with the Limbic-Self feelings of recognition and belonging, and I am again reassured that I, or my self, exists.

Remember, this self I am recognizing is a series of levels of organizations of selves, and it is the continuity of these many levels and moments of selves that is at any given moment experienced so reassuringly. Here is the argument, most of which is now repetitious. But be forewarned, my argument may not be totally reassuring.

The self is made up of many components, but the lowest level components, the Cerebral-Self and the Limbic-Self, when operating at a low level of integration, are capable of processing much of the incoming stimulation and, thereby, maintaining the organization of the organism. At this level of integration, what we usually think of as ourselves, the Functional-Self or the Self-Aware-Self, exists only as a potential. When we are asleep or when we are operating on a reflexive or habitual level, the self, as we are accustomed to thinking of it, does not exist. In other words, the self does not exist when the components of the self are not *integrated*. This is analogous to saying that salt does not exist when the sodium and chloride in a salt molecule have been separated into elements. Or, the physical human being does not exist when the life-maintaining physical components of the body have been dismembered. An integration, a synthesis between the Cerebral-Self and the Limbic-Self, is a *moment* of consciousness and only a momentary experience of self. When the next higher level of integration of the central nervous system occurs, and the focus of consciousness becomes one's immediate past experience of having been conscious of one's thoughts or feelings, then one is in the Self-Aware-Self. Now, at that moment, we *seem to know* that we have a self.

But here's the problem that philosophers have raised. This is not a case of the self knowing that the self has a self; it is that knowledge, that consciousness of the self, that *is* the self. In other words, nothing in this argument proves that we are a separate self experiencing this continuity of moments of selves. We are, once again, just the experiences of self.

Well, at least we aren't infinitely regressing. If you have accepted the necessity of avoiding the dilemma of infinite regression, then this concept of the self may be somewhat palatable. Moreover, as the moments of consciousness proceed one after another, or as mentation relative to your self continues, there is at least a reassuring *continuity* in the experience of yourself, however illusory it might be. In other words, when you are feeling yourself for more than just a moment, and that continuity of feelings is the old familiar you, *that* is the self you want to hold on to, and it certainly *feels* real.

The feeling of realness not withstanding, logic dictates, following this argument, that if you are no more than the occurrence of a series of moments of synthesis between thoughts and feelings, than you cannot exist, outside of that process, to guide the process. How can you guide the process when you are nothing but the process?

The Primacy of Feelings

So, following Descartes, you exist because you think. But Descartes' reasoning was circular, so you don't exist to know that you exist, you just exist. Your existence is you. But what about that wonderful feeling? I submit that in identifying and being yourself, feeling is primary. Yes, at that moment of consciousness when the Self-Aware-Self exists many self-concepts regarding your self are being activated in the Invested-Self, but it is the enduring limbic system feelings of familiarity and belonging that reassures you even before you label the feeling with such self-concepts as your name and your profession.

Does this mean that we should change "I think; therefore, I am." to "I feel; therefore, I am."? No, these moments and upper levels of self, from consciousness to the Transcendent-Self, are always feelings plus thoughts. But I am suggesting that in thinking and theorizing about your self, you should focus more on the feelings than on the thoughts. My reasoning is that, as far as understanding and treating the self, understanding the feelings of and about self will be more productive than understanding the thoughts.

See how you feel about this. At this very moment, do you have any doubts about who you are? I hope and assume not. When I asked that question, did you reassure yourself by immediately identify yourself by thinking of your name?

My guess is, no. Even before you thought of your name you already *felt* that you were yourself. You didn't even have to name yourself. But suppose you didn't instantly get that reassuring feeling of self. Suppose, even after you named yourself, the name wasn't meaningful, there was no feeling of familiarity associated with the name. How then would you feel? My guess is, disconcerted or perhaps even panicked. My guess is you would be very motivated to act very quickly to recovering that familiar feeling. Furthermore, my guess is, this is the way the psychotic feels, or anyone else who is for any length of time "not feeling himself."

A Practical Resolution of the Mind-Brain Problem by Making One More Assumption

Does this mean we have resolved the mind-brain problem? Hardly. No one else has. Why should I expect to? I am only saying that even if you must still only *assume* you have consciousness and a self, focusing on your feelings as well as your thoughts will nevertheless give you more control over your self if you do actually exist.

Let me elaborate on this assumption. This reassuring feeling of self is enabled by a continuity of moments of consciousness. During those moments, my focus on the self-concepts associated with my self in my Self-Concepts-Self is giving me the feeling that I exist and that I am at that moment a self that is aware of my self. Good for me; I'm happy. There is still the problem, however, that no one else can know for sure that I exist and that I am contemplating my existence. Furthermore, *I* have no way of knowing that anyone else exists, outside of my brain's neuronal activity. This is the dilemma philosophers have gleefully raised in the past. Even if, though unproven, I do exist, everyone and everything else in the universe might only exist in my mind, and maybe I only exist in the mind of God.

Even worse, perhaps I only exist in your mind, and all these clever thoughts I'm writing are yours, not mine. Even my illusory self doesn't like that.

Here's my resolution of this dilemma. I've asked you to make a number of assumptions, beginning with the assumption that life for whatever reason evolved from non-living matter, and that the experience we call the self evolved eventually from that event. Now I'm am asking you to assume that you and I are not one experience, that you and I are two separated being who ultimately evolved from that initial event, two not entirely unique individuals who now are experiencing similar feelings that we identify as our selves. It follows from this assumption that others, including those who may identify themselves as counselees, are also separate selves capable of experiencing the feelings of being and examining themselves.

Now, from this essential assumption, everything else I propose in this book can have validity.

Freewill? Only If You Are Conscious

But here is another disconcerting feeling. If you are not just an illusion, if you do exist and are capable of examining your existence, can you also guide yourself? That is, do you have *freewill?*

The controversy regarding freewill can be simple stated. Most lay people assume that they make their own choices. They assume that if they lift their arms, it is because they *decided* to life their arms. On the other hand, philosophers through the ages have questioned the assumption of freewill. Their argument has been that human behavior is *predetermined* by such factors as human genetics, previous experience, related environmental conditions, or God. Given all these interacting variables, specific human behavior *will* occur. The fact that people *decide* to lift their arms is superfluous. It had already been decided by these other factors that the arms would be lifted. So-called "conscious decisions" were merely after-the-fact statements of the *predetermined* and inevitable.

This philosophical position, however logical, is repugnant to most people. There is the humorous story about Ralph Waldo Emerson. Emerson was being escorted, in a minister's carriage, to the minister's church to give a lecture. The minister was a proponent of predestination, a theological position that questions human freewill. When the minister, in pushing his argument for predestination, stated, "See, Mr. Emerson, it was obviously predestined that you would come and speak at my church this morning," Emerson jumped out of the carriage and walked back home.

Unfortunately, Emerson's behavior, however dramatic, does not prove the case of freewill. Given Emerson's argumentative personality, his resistive behavior could well have been predetermined by his personality development. Likewise, the physiological and psychological speculations thus far offered in this book have not seemed to support the concept of freewill. Much of the organization of the central nervous system is preestablished by genetics and then further complexity in that organization is created by experience and learning. When a situation demanding a decision impinges upon the central nervous system, in the form of a pattern of excitation, there is usually a neuron assembly sensitive to that pattern that will coordinate a predictable set of motor-behaviors or stimulate a series of mentations. Even when there is no neuron assembly sensitive to the exact incoming pattern of stimulation, and consciousness is required to facilitate the search for equivalent neuron assemblies, consciousness has not been described as an instrument of freewill but rather as an instrument for refining and allowing a decision that is *generally* determined by the existing components in the nervous system. "Generally," as used here, means in a *predetermined* range.

We will be assisted in our analysis of the question of freewill, how-ever, if we start by offering definitions of the term. Consider this defini-tion: **Freewill** *is freedom from cause and effect.* Scientific theory and research is based upon the assumption of cause and effect. Freewill, by this definition, would mean that, given a verified cause, we may freely *will* another effect other than indicated by the cause. But, given this def-inition, when do we exercise our "freewill?" Certainly, given the limita-tions of our heavy-muscled, heavy-boned physiognomy, and the gravitational forces on this planet, we may not freely will ourselves to fly effortlessly through the air, unassisted by mechanical devices. In other words, the assumption is made that we cannot violate the physical laws of the universe.

But it has also been argued that life itself is a violation of the phys-ical laws of the universe. The natural physical order of the universe is entropy, or the tendency of physical matter to become disorganized. Life has been defined as an organization that is motivated to main-tain and enhance its organization. Hence, *life* violates natural physi-cal law. As such, to continue to live might be thought of as a continual act of freewill.

But such a concept of "freewill" seems to beg the question. In the human organism, the chain of events from a threat to a life-maintaining response is cause and effect. Whatever caused that initial rebellion against the natural laws of the universe, once life existed, its behavior followed physical laws even though that first moment of life may have violate the law of entropy. Therefore, nowadays and long after that ini-tial moment of life we are still left with the uncomfortable situation of apparently having no freewill. Moreover, not only does such a conclu-sion leave us with no control over our decisions, it also makes us un-responsible for our decisions. That might not be so bad, but it also makes others un-responsible to us.

So perhaps our first definition of freewill was unnecessarily limit-ing; it may also have been misleading. Freedom from cause and effect is impossible not only because it is a violation of natural law but also because our interpretation of this definition seemed to imply that there is a *choice*. As you recall, the statement, "I choose," leads us into infinite regression. Who chooses within the chooser? But if instead that "I choose" is understood to mean "I am the process of choosing," in the sense that the choosing *is* the self, just as consciousness is the self, then the following operational and logical definition of freewill may be possible.

Freewill *is the experience of choosing, the experience of the self at the moment of ambiguity associated with the absence of an automatic self-sustaining response and the resolution of that ambiguity in the feeling of "recognition" of a "generally" acceptable and probably effective mentation or motor response.* By this definition, freewill exists for human beings in the same sense that consciousness exists. Both occur as processes of the self. Both potentially contribute to the maintenance and further integration of the organization of the self. Consciousness makes possible a greater variety of cell assemblies. *Freewill, now defined as the process of choosing one cell assembly over another, must occur if integration is to continue.*

Freewill, as defined, is only possible if consciousness is occurring, and *consciousness only occurs if automatic self-integrating responses are not occurring* or if there is a history of positive affect associated with consciousness making consciousness a preferred ongoing process. As such, freewill is *not* a violation of cause and effect. Cause and effect is still operating as a description of the sequence of events, even in the fine discriminations taking place when one "generally" better fit is being made between an incoming signal and one of thousands of cerebral cortex cell assemblies. The existence of a self is always *caused* by antecedent events. But *the most effective cell assemblies would not be chosen without the event of consciousness, or the Functional-Self, as well as the antecedent events that established the self as an integrated organization capable of enduring the ambiguity of "freewill" long enough for the most self-serving response to be chosen.*

But even this explanation might not fully satisfy the desire to know that one is capable of choosing. What we want to experience is still *"I choose,"* not *"I am the process of choosing,"* just as what we want to experienced is "I am conscious" rather than "I am consciousness." The concern is probably one of giving up something, of losing a degree of control. But the fact is, whatever choice is made was made because of your uniqueness. Your unique self is the cause of your choice. The fact that the incoming stimulus was not available in your Cerebral-Self made it necessary for your Functional-Self to operate and make possible the variety of cell assemblies from which only one eventually integrated with the efferent cell assembly that effected your choice. The fact that your unique self had developed and exists in its current state is the primary event, among all antecedent events, that eventuated in your choice. *Given all the other factors operating, in being your unique self, your choice was inevitable, not because it was beyond your control but because you are the control. In this sense, and without violating cause and effect, you choose—and you therefore demonstrate freewill.*

By this definition of freewill, it must be acknowledged that most of the time human beings do not demonstrate freewill. Most of the time, even the most integrated individuals operate on reflexive or habitual behaviors. Most of our time, even most of our waking hours, we are not even operating on the level of our Functional-Selves. In other words, most of the time we are not even conscious. *Therefore, by our new definition, freewill as well as consciousness are the exceptions and not the rule in human experience.*

Finally, here is an even less stringent definition of freewill, one that almost reaches the level of an operational or measurable definition. **Freewill** *is occurring when the preponderance of factors predisposing a behavior is internal to the organism rather than external.* This definition does not deny the causal effect of the past on the present; antecedent experiences have obviously created present potential for behavior. But freewill is possible because current choices are made on the basis of *immediate* causes. By this definition, freewill is occurring when the antecedent events have created within the organism the potential for determining the nature and the occurrences or the lack of occurrences of the behavior, even though the current triggering of that behavior might have been an external event.

By this definition, there can be two kinds of freewill: conscious choice and habitual choice. As in the previous definition, this explanation of freewill is only acceptable if one has already accepted the existence of consciousness. In conscious choice, the complex integration of the central nervous system that is consciousness, or the Functional-Self, is the preponderant internal predisposing factor determining behavior. That is to say, there is a lot more going on inside the organism than mere stimulus-response or reflex arc, and the varieties of behaviors that might occur cannot be determined by the external event. *The operation of consciousness determines the behavior.*

In habitual choice, knowledge of the external event might enable an accurate prediction of the eventual behavior of the organism, but if the *unique* antecedent conscious choices of the organism have operated to create a habit that functions in the best interest of the organism then it may be said that it is the internal factors that are predominantly determining the organism's behavior and not the external triggering event, and therefore freewill is occurring.

In summary, by this definition, freewill is occurring when the organism, through immediate consciousness or through the past effects of consciousness, is guiding its own destiny.

Responsibility Nonetheless

By either of these less stringent definitions of freewill, *you are also responsible for your choices.* Responsibility, of course, implies responsibility in relation to something else. As a living being, you are responsible to your sovereign motivation to maintain and enhance your living organization. As a human being with a highly integrated central nervous system and a self, you are responsible for maintaining and enhancing your self. The term **responsibility** *can now be defined as the resolution of the ambiguity of freewill in the service of continuing integration of the self,* and **irresponsibility** *is choosing to behave in ways that lead to disintegration of the self.*

For human beings, irresponsibility is also generally associated with impulsive immediate-gratification seeking behavior. Highly integrated human beings can automatically process a vast majority of incoming stimuli. When a disruptive stimulus is encountered, consciousness is required to make possible a variety of cell assemblies so that the most effective fit can be made between the incoming stimulus and problem-solving mentation or motor behavior. Impulsive responses seek immediate relief from the anxiety associated with the disorganizing stimulus, and they short circuit the search for the most effective response.

More integrated selves usually experience success in the use of consciousness in problem-solving. Therefore, they have developed an association between the limbic system feeling of *enduring* delayed gratification and the belief that problems can be resolved. Therefore, when confronted with the ambiguity of freewill, Integrated-Selves value "enduring" rather than *immediate* anxiety-reduction.

Now let us consider our previous question. Given these definitions of freewill and responsibility, can you now *feel* somewhat more comfortable with the definition of consciousness that says consciousness is merely a moment of synthesis of thoughts and feelings? At this moment, as you read these words, to the extent that you comprehend what you are reading, you are conscious. You are operating at the level of integration of your central nervous system that I have labeled the Functional-Self. If, the next moment, you let your mind lapse and no thoughts or other forms of mentation are occurring, you are no longer conscious, and your Functional-Self does not at that moment exist. You self is functioning at a lower level of integration, and what you ordinarily think of as your self exists only as potential. If, on the other hand, these words stimulate you to rise to the level of integration that has been labeled the Self-Aware-Self, and your own ongoing mentation is the focus of your consciousness, this level of cerebral cortex integration is associated with the limbic system feeling of belongingness, and the total experience is one of reassurance that your self does in fact exist.

Moreover, at those times when your Functional-Self and your Self-Aware-Self are not operating, you are obviously not conscious of the passage of time. Therefore, when you are not operating at the level of integration of the Functional-Self or the Self-Aware-Self, you have no recollection of those absences in functioning, and therefore there is no lapse of awareness of self to undermine the reassuring experience of continuity in your self.

If, while in the state of self-awareness, an event occurs in your environment that is a potential threat to the maintenance of your human organization, two general choices are possible, both of which demonstrate freewill: there is behavior that demonstrates the opposite of responsibility, and there is behavior that demonstrates responsibility. The potential threat to your organization impinges upon the central nervous system and temporarily reduces its level of organization. This results in activation of the limbic system feeling of "anxiety." The behavior that demonstrates irresponsibility would be some form of behavior that either capitulates to the threat immediately or that tends to reduce the painful anxiety while doing nothing to combat the potential threat. The behavior that demonstrates responsibility would be consciousness in the service of meeting the challenge of the threat, by facilitating the cerebral cortex reintegration into new patterns of integration that would coordinate behavior to meet the challenge of the threat. In other words, if in the face of a threat, you consciously focus on that threat and are in active pursuit of a solution to that threat, you are acting with freewill *and* with responsibility.

But there might still be the inclination to ask, did you choose to be responsible, or was responsibility merely the effect of all the causes that preceded the responsible behavior? The form of the question is of course a trap. By asking the question that way, you are thrown once again into the problem of infinite regression. The responsible behavior, as defined, did occur, and that responsible behavior would not have occurred had the unique organization that is your self not existed. The existence of your *unique* self is the cause that resulted in the effect of your responsibility. Because your complex and highly integrated central nervous system exists at the level of the Functional-Self, the behavioral options that will be generated by your consciousness also may exist. This increased number of options, or degrees of freedom to behave, would not exist unless your unique self exists. The "choice" of responsibility was made because *you* exist. However, if the elaborate cell assembly in your cerebral cortex that represents the sentence, "I choose," is associated with more of the limbic system feeling of comfort than the cell assembly that represents "is choosing," then continue to let that cell assembly be the focus of your consciousness. The result is the same either way. *As long as the choice is made to be rather than not-to-be, your behavior is a demonstration of freewill and responsibility.*

Positive and Negative States and Processes of the Self

Even when we are struggling to be responsible, we might falter and behave irresponsibly. That is, we might choose to have immediate reduction in anxiety rather than endure the anxiety so as to continue enhancing our organization. Sometimes this might be necessary as when the pain of facing the challenge of growth is too much to endure. But if this is more than just a sometimes choice, the over indulgence in this choice might necessitate the intervention of a psychotherapist to aid in the more effective use of consciousness to assist the person overcome this ineffective habit. Understanding of positive and negative states and processes of the self will assist in that therapeutic process.

"Unconsciousness" and Subconsciousness

It will help us to understand the functioning of the self if we further categorize the self into "self-states" and "self-process" The term **self-state** *refers to a specified point along the continuum of self-integration.* The term refers to something that is static. The only actually static state of the central nervous system is death. Except when dead, you are never static. You are, however, always in the process of functioning around one of those hypothetical points along the continuum of self-development. Self-states *are hypothetical states that are defined for convenience of conceptualization.*

The Limbic-Self, the Cerebral-Self, the Invested-Self, the Self-Concepts-Self, and the Integrated-Self are all such states of the self. The information stored at those various levels of integration of the self exists as potential, as a state of readiness to be activated. There are also other common states of the self that need to be defined. The term **unconscious** has two meanings, both of which are states of the self. Unconscious *means asleep, or a relatively dormant, low-level of activity of the cerebral cortex and arousal activation from the limbic system.* The second meaning of unconscious is the classical **psychoanalytic unconscious.** *Stripped of all of its psychoanalytic theoretical relevance, this state of the self merely refers to poorly integrated cell assemblies in the cerebral cortex that may be part of either the Cerebral-Self or the Invested-Self.* Since these cell assemblies are poorly integrated with other cell assemblies or with the limbic system, they are not readily activated by the Functional-Self. In the conscious or awake state, other better integrated cerebral cell assemblies dominate cerebral cortex activity. When the individual is asleep, however, and external stimulation is reduced, these less integrated cerebral cell assemblies may be activated by strong limbic system activity. The result is a dream state in which the "unconscious" cell assemblies or memories are activated and express themselves in a somewhat chaotic, alogical fashion, and thus require interpretation by the Psychoanalyst.

The terms **subconsciousness or the subconscious state** *are merely other terms for the Cerebral-Self. "Subconscious" information is information available for activation by external stimulation or through the mediation of consciousness but information that is not currently the focus of consciousness.*

Esthetic, rapturous, and ethereal states are variations of the Limbic-Self. These are states in which there is relatively more activity in the limbic system than there is in the cerebral cortex. Thus, these are states in which the feelings are powerful and the thoughts are temporarily suppressed and relatively inadequate to describe the intense feelings.

There are also pathological states of the self that refer to damage or disruption in the organism's neuroanatomy or neurophysiology, as in brain damaged or in psychotic patients.

The term **self-process** *refers to interaction between components of the self.* The major self-processes are the Functional-Self, otherwise known as the conscious process, and the Self-Aware-Self. As it has been described, consciousness is the synthesis or interaction between specific cell assemblies in the cerebral cortex and the limbic system feeling of "recognition," usually associated with other limbic system feelings. The Self-Aware-Self is the process of focusing on the self through the medium of consciousness. The terms unconscious process and subconscious *process* are misnomers. Whatever the level of integration of the cerebral cortex cell assemblies, when these cell assemblies are activated and there is interaction with the limbic system feeling of recognition then there is a moment of consciousness. Even though this recognition might be vague, or in a dream, it is still a moment of consciousness. To call a moment of consciousness "unconsciousness" is a linguistic absurdity. It is much more logical to think of the unconscious and the subconscious as levels of relative integration of cerebral cell assemblies and try to be consistent in using the term consciousness as a process rather than as a state.

Positive and Negative Self-States

In general, states and processes are positive if they contribute to the continued maintenance and further integration of the human organism. States and processes are negative if they impede or undermine the continued maintenance and further integration of the organization of the organism. When the Cerebral-Self or the Invested-Self has insufficient information to provide effective coordination to cope with threatening stimulation then these are negative states of the Cerebral-Self and the Invested-Self. When the self-concepts are inadequately articulated, or in conflict, this is a negative state of the Self-Concepts-Self. A negative state of the Limbic-Self is activation of any unpleasant feeling. As described thus far, the Integrated-Self has no negative state.

Positive states of the Cerebral-Self and the Invested-Self occur when there is adequate information available to cope with threatening stimulation. A positive state of the Self-Concepts-Self exists when there is enough articulation and integration of the self-concepts to facilitate problem-solving. When the level of integration of the self-concepts reaches this degree, however, it is more appropriate to label this state as an Integrated-Self.

Positive Self-Processes

Positive and negative self-processes are numerous, and it will assist our understanding of the functioning of the self to describe these various processes in greater detail.

By its very nature, consciousness is a positive process. Consciousness, in freeing the cerebral cortex from the inhibition associated with focusing behavior, enables further integration of the cerebral cortex. Therefore, the more time one spends being conscious, the greater the probability that one will increase one's self-integration. But the activation of the cerebral cortex cell assemblies made possible by consciousness may also be associated with unpleasant feelings, located in the limbic system. Therefore, though consciousness may not always make cowards of us all, there are time when the process of consciousness activates such unpleasant feelings that we might just as soon not be conscious. It is because of this potential for consciousness to activate either pleasant or unpleasant limbic system feelings that we have developed numerous mechanisms for managing these pleasant or unpleasant consequences, many of which are counterproductive in the long run.

Mentation-For-the-Sake-of-Mentation is a positive self-process. Daydreaming, reading, listening to music, and viewing art all involve mentation that may be indulged in for no other reason than the fact that the process of mentation is associated with pleasurable limbic system feelings. The most positive by-product of this process is further integration of other cerebral cell assemblies of the Invested-Self. Another possible positive outcome of mentation-for-the-sake-of-mentation is temporary reduction of debilitating negative affect. When there is disruptive stimulation impinging upon the central nervous system, the most effective behavior is immediate problem-solving. Frequently, however, immediate problem-solving is not possible. If the disruptive stimulation is not life-threatening and can be temporarily ignored, mentation-for-the-sake-of-mentation may assist in re-establishing a functional level of integration of the central nervous system by stimulating limbic system feelings that are incompatible with the anxiety associated with the disruptive stimulation. Then, in the less disrupted state, problem-solving may eventually be possible.

Non-Cerebral Activation of Positive Limbic System States Pleasurable feelings in the limbic system may be activated in ways other than through mentation. Physical activity, massage, and sensual and sexual stimulation are self-processes that may activate positive limbic system affect. All such activities, of course, have representation in the cerebral cortex, but in these processes there is relatively more activation in the limbic system than in the cerebral cortex.

Self-Suspension. Another way of managing disruptive stimulation, so as to allow the body to function more effectively and also to reduce the random activity in the cerebral cortex associated with excessive unpleasant limbic system activity, is self-suspension. Self-suspension goes by many names: meditation, relaxation, progressive relaxation, transcendental meditation, yoga, etc. In all of these activities there is focus on non-stimulating mentation or reduced mentation so that the associated limbic system affect will be neither positive nor negative, but essentially neutral. Even those processes of self-suspension that do require the mediation of consciousness have as their intention the creation of the limbic system state of serenity, of affective neutrality. In these forms of self-suspension, the focusing of consciousness is used to reduce activity in both the limbic system and in the cerebral cortex. After some degree of self-suspension has been obtained, and mentation recommences, the resulting reduction in random firing of cerebral cortex cell assemblies enables the Functional-Self to proceed more efficiently with problem-solving. In other words, through the use of the process of self-suspension, there is greater centering-of-self.

Negative Self-Processes and The Psychological Coping Mechanisms

Psychological coping mechanisms are *generally* negative self-processes. They are relatively permanent components of the Invested-Self that occur habitually when anxiety is experienced. Psychological coping mechanisms reduce the anxiety, but then the anxiety fails to motivate problem-solving. Therefore, psychological coping mechanisms, to one degree or another, reduce the probability that the source of the anxiety will be altered and self-integration will proceed.

But psychological coping mechanisms sometimes function like positive self-processes. This occurs when the disruptive stimulation is severe, and is eventually removed by something other than the self. In such cases, psychological coping mechanisms might have enabled the self to avoid being overwhelmed by anxiety until the non-self agent intervened. But, in general, psychological coping mechanisms interfere with the further integration of the self, and therefore psychological coping mechanisms are for the most part negative self-processes.

Here are some of the common psychological coping mechanisms and how they may be understood as negative self-processes. **Denial** *is the failure to respond to a threat*. People using the psychological coping mechanism of denial act as though they are totally unaware of a stimulus that others assume should be threatening. Denial is said to occur at a subconscious level and is to be differentiated from **suppression,** *which is the conscious choice not to focus on a threat.* The natural human central nervous system response to a threatening or disorganizing stimulus is the use of consciousness to disinhibit the cerebral cortex and increase the probability of creating an effective response to the threat. At times, this otherwise effective response may be relatively ineffective because it is not timely or convenient to attack a particular threat. The choice of suppression, or choosing not to focus on that threat but rather to focus on a more immediately manageable or demanding threat will be more efficient and in intended to allow the person to eventually confront the less demanding threat.

For the person with a history of being relatively ineffective in the use of consciousness, a situation that is common with children, consciousness might increase the disorganizing effect of the threatening stimulus, and denial might serve the same function as suppression. In this denier, a mildly disruptive stimulus might cause the denier to focus on the stimulus, without recognizing it, until a stronger competing stimulus disrupts the focus. If the strong competing focus is not also anxiety-provoking then consciousness of the new stimulus can occur. If, in the mean time, the anxiety-provoking stimulus goes away on its own then denial has protected the individual during that time. On the other hand, if the anxiety-provoking stimulus continues to increase, total disruption of the central nervous system organization may occur, and the individual may faint and thereby also escape the anxiety.

In denial, no cerebral cell assembly or representation of the threatening stimulus is ever formed. *In the psychological coping mechanism of* **repression,** *consciousness of the threatening stimulus has occurred in the past, and there already exists a cerebral cortex cell assembly representing the threatening stimulus.* When this existing cerebral cell assembly is activated by an incoming stimulus, the effective response would be either an habitual motor-defense against the threat, or consciousness. The person who develops the habit of repression has been relatively ineffective in past uses of consciousness. Therefore, when there is no habitual effective defense against the disruptive incoming stimulus, the same mechanism used by the denier is used by the repressor. Focus, without recognition, remains on the disruptive cell assembly, and consciousness is deferred until another incoming stimulus diverts the focusing behavior and consciousness can occur regarding the new, non threatening stimulus. The difference between denial and repression is that, in repression, the anxiety-provoking stimulus is a part of the self. It does not go away. Moreover, the anxiety provoking cerebral cortex cell assembly, or memory, is likely to be related to numerous other cell assemblies, and therefore subject to frequent reactivation. Therefore, the person with the habit of repression, in being unable to effectively integrate the repressed memory, remains in a chronic low-level state of anxiety.

The failure to employ consciousness to integrate repressed memories may underlie the development of a number of other psychological coping mechanisms. A person may use **obsessive thinking or compulsive behavior** *as learned responses to the anxiety provoked by the repressed memory.* The obsessive thinking or compulsive behavior activates associated limbic system feelings that are to some degree incompatible with the limbic system feeling of anxiety. Consciousness is employed in obsessive thinking or compulsive behavior, not to solve the problem that is the source of the anxiety, but rather to repetitively "recognize" the obsessive thoughts and the thoughts associated with the compulsive behavior. This relatively less anxiety-provoking obsessive/compulsive mentation is continually activated, reducing the probability that the more disruptive anxiety-provoking cell assembly will be activated.

Depression, *like other psychological coping mechanisms, is only partially effective in reducing anxiety.* The memory that triggers the defense of depression is the memory of a significant loss. When you have identified with another person, object, or experience, that cell assembly has become a part of your Invested-Self. Therefore, when that something is lost, it as a part of your self that is lost. The loss of a part of one's self disrupts the organization of the self, and anxiety results. The natural response to this disorganization is an attempt to reintegrate or re-establish a new organization. This reintegration requires time, and during that time anxiety must be endured. *The anxiety associated with a loss is termed* **grief.** Grief is tolerated by most people, and the grief-anxiety goes away when the self is reorganized to exclude the lost object. *For the person who has a poorly integrated self or who has suffered a series of losses that have drastically disorganized the self,* **the habit of depression** may develop. Depression reduces the intensity of the grief by reorganizing the self at a lower level of integration. In grief, a certain amount of suppression is necessary. The grieving person may wisely choose not to think about the loss. This enables the person to continue functioning. But suppression, practiced too frequently, might become repression, as the choice of not-thinking becomes overlearned and automatic. Not thinking about that which is lost not only cuts the person off from the anxiety associated with that loss, it also makes unavailable to the Functional-Self all of those pleasurable feelings associated with that which has been lost. Moreover, something that was of great significance to a person is integrated in numerous ways with other aspects of the self. Therefore, access to these other aspects of the self and their associated pleasurable feelings is also lost. Pleasurable affect, in general, is reduced. Since the Functional-Self is reduced, the ongoing capacity to increase self-integration is reduced, and other sources of positive affect are less available. This is the anhedonia associated with depression.

As unpleasant as depression might be, for some people it may not be as unpleasant as the anxiety associated with the initial loss. Then, once a person has learned this depressive response, the person may habitually respond with depression to offset the anxiety associated with less significant inevitable losses that occur throughout life.

A person using the psychological coping mechanism of **rationalization** *avoids the anxiety associated with a potential disorganization of a self-concept.* This is another case in which consciousness is subverted in the service of the immediate reduction of anxiety. When information inconsistent with the self-concept impinges upon the central nervous system of the rationalizer, anxiety is provoked. The rationalizer's experience with consciousness has been impaired, and the positive feelings associated with "recognition" are not strong enough to offset the anxiety associated with the incoming information. This anxiety, however, is not so overwhelming as to cause repression or denial. Rather, consciousness continues, and cerebral cortex associations are made, but the only cerebral cortex cell assemblies that can be activated are those that have strong enough positive associations with the limbic system to offset the anxiety. Since "recognition" and its generally positive associations in the limbic system are relatively weak in rationalizers, their Functional-Selves cannot continue the search for a cell assembly that is compatible with the incoming stimulation. Therefore, a less problem-solving effective but more flattering anxiety-reducing cell assembly is activated, and the rationalizers think positive rather than negative thoughts about themselves.

Projection *is the habit of attributing responsibility for one's feelings or thoughts to some agent outside of the self.* A disorganizing stimulus, usually in the form of information that conflicts with a self-concept, impinges upon the Invested-Self. An effective non projective reorganization of the Invested-Self would be one that results from a synthesis of this new information with existing information so that the new information does not continue to be disruptive. For example, my self-concept is that I am intelligent, but the new information is that I have done poorly on a math test. This new information would *not* continue to be disruptive if I also have the self-concept that I am just a beginning math student, and I have hitherto been making steady progress. People who habitually use projection, however, have developed a way of almost immediately integrating disruptive information into the Invested-Self. They have developed a generalization or, on the neurological level, a lambda system, that can fit with any disorganizing threat to the

Invested-Self. The disrupting information activates a pattern of search for any other lambda system, except those that are a part of the Invested-Self, that are associated with anxiety-reducing feelings from the limbic system. The thoughts that the test was unfair, that the teacher is punitive, that the test was mis-scored are all relatively less anxiety-provoking than the thought that I am stupid. Therefore, I am inclined to focus on those "projective thoughts".

In projection, as with all psychological coping mechanisms, the anxiety-reduction is only partial. The reassuring projective thoughts usually run counter to other information about the non-self agent that the projector would like to believe. So, typically, the projector must expend more effort looking for other evidence to support the original projection. *The extreme overuse of the habit of projection, resulting in an integration of an accumulation of related projective thoughts, is the* **paranoid process, or paranoia.**

Negative Self-Concepts

All of these psychological coping mechanisms are indications of impaired or reduced functioning of a Functional-Self that has learned ways of reducing anxiety rather than the use of consciousness to solve the problem presented by the disruptive stimulus. These psychological coping mechanisms, when only occasionally employed, are merely inefficient methods of coping, and might therefore be relatively small components of a Cerebral or Invested-Self. A potentially more debilitating negative self-process involves those self-concepts that make up that major component of the Invested-Self, the Self-Concept-Self. Negative Self-Concepts develop when the Functional-Self has *habitually* failed to cope with disorganizing stimulation. When this happens, the abstraction of the Invested-Self that is the Self-Concept-Self might become associated with a negative limbic system feeling, such as "inadequacy," "disgust," "hatred," "depression," or general anxiety.

Therefore, whenever the person rises to the level of self-integration of the Self-Aware-Self, this learned negative feeling is activated. In order to avoid these learned negative feelings, it might be necessary for such a person to avoid thinking about his or her self. Naturally, this avoidance of the Self-Aware-Self impedes further integration of the self. But avoidance of the Self-Aware-Self may also require a considerable investment of time and effort. Constant denial or repression might be required to prevent the consciousness from focusing on any aspect of the self, and constant denial and repression would leave the person functioning only at a reflexive or habitual level. Therefore, a person with a negative self-concept may develop the use of even more self-destructive techniques to distort or reduce self-awareness—paranoia, alcoholism, drug abuse, or suicide.

You will recall that self-concepts are abstractions of many components of the Invested-Self. They are states of the organization of the central nervous system; they are not processes. As abstractions, however, self-concepts process efficiently with limbic system excitation. The cell assembly containing the abstraction is housed in the cerebral cortex, and therefore is neither negative nor positive. It is the integration with the limbic system that assigns the self-concept its positive or negative value. Self-concepts that are integrated with negative feelings are negative self-concepts, and self-concepts that are integrated with positive feelings are positive self-concepts. As abstractions, self-concepts are efficiently brought to consciousness. As a concept, the self-concept relates to numerous aspects of the Invested-Self. Therefore, a self-concept with a negative value places a negative value on many aspects of the Invested-Self. While there are many self-concepts, there is also a generalized concept of these concepts. This concept-of-concepts is what the Self-Aware-Self is focusing on when you ask yourself the question, "Am I a worthwhile person?". Some people generally feel and believe that they are worthwhile, others generally feel and believe that they are not. Theoretically, it may be possible for a person to have all negative self-concepts and therefore be an integrated *negative* person. In actuality, this is not possible. In order for a person to survive, probably the majority of that person's physical actions and mentations must be effective. Therefore, the person *will* have positive self-concepts. However, it is the combination of these positive self-concepts and the negative self-concepts that have been acquired through ineffective experience that leaves the self-concepts in conflict and the person far short of being an Integrated-Self.

The person who is approaching self-integration will also have some negative self-concepts. But the Functional-Self will be operating to more effectively integrate the self, thereby reducing these negative self-concepts. But, the person whose general self-concept is relatively negative will likely be avoiding the Self-Aware-Self, and therefore have difficulty in overcoming negative self-concepts and moving on the next level of self-development, the Transcendent-Self.

Transcending the Self

The Reified I

The human self evolved as a more efficient method of enabling the human organism to maintain and enhance its organization. As the self becomes more integrated, the human being's capacity to cope with disruptive and threatening stimulation is increased, and the probability of the human organism's survival increases correspondingly. But, although the self is an effective instrument, the self is not a perfect instrument. It has built-in liabilities. The complex integration of the cerebral cortex and the limbic system that makes the self possible also makes possible negative self-concepts. Less evolved animals are not burdened with the chronic negative feelings that are associated with such concepts. Less evolved animals do not have to control such feelings with techniques such as less than effective coping mechanism that turn out to be self-defeating or self-destructive. Most tellingly, animals do not intentionally commit suicide. Even the ideal self, the Integrated-Self, has a built-in liability. The Integrated-Self can become too integrated within itself and cease to have reason for being. This excessively self-contained self is one possible development in what I will term, the Reified-I.

As the Functional-Self continually differentiates the Invested-Self from the larger Cerebral-Self, it is the uniqueness of this integrated organization that makes it efficient. The greater the differentiation of the Invested-Self from the Cerebral-Self the more readily the familiar and non-threatening stimulation is processed. The human organism is therefore capable of handling greater complexity in the external environment.

This greater organization and integration of this increasingly unique Invested-Self makes possible the differentiation of the self from complex external stimulation. When the Functional-Self is then called on to assist in the processing of this complex external stimulation, more refined generalizations are made and more sophisticated abstractions of these generalizations are created. This means that relatively more mentation must occur. Since the self is already efficiently handling most immediate threats to the organism's organization, this highly complex external stimulation is usually not an immediate threat to the organism. Therefore, prolonged mentation, with the flow of moments of recognition, results in a flow of successes in processing the information. The limbic system affect associated with the experience of recognition is generally positive and makes consciousness and mentation an ever-increasing positive experience. For the most part, therefore, the increasingly complex and integrated Invested-Self that is being created by this inward focusing mentational process is an all the more positive experience because of its uniqueness. The general feeling of "familiarity" associated with this unique Invested-Self is the "I" experience, the sense of identity that is instantly recognized in the Self-Aware-Self. After the Invested-Self has been sufficiently differentiated from the Cerebral-Self, this "I" feeling becomes so associated with the effectiveness of the self-process that it is the ultimate abstraction of the self. Although you may have many abstract cognitive labels with which you identify your self—your name, your nationality, your occupation—it is the *feeling* of familiarity activated in your limbic system that is most valued. If that familiar feeling of the "I" does not occur, however vaguely, to the Self-Aware-Self, there is an immediate surge of anxiety. This feeling of familiarity, this "I" feeling, is so valued that it is the standard whereby all other experiences are judged. Once the "I" feeling is established, through sufficient differentiation of the Invested-Self from the Cerebral-Self, it becomes **Reified.** That is, *it is an abstraction that is so familiar and so significant, it becomes as though a real, concrete thing. This abstraction that is experienced as absolutely real, as the* *essence of the self, is the* **Reified I.** Yet, the Reified I, however real its experience, *is* still an abstraction, a complex organization of neurons in the central nervous system, an organization of neurons that is readily activated but, nevertheless, just an organization of neurons. It does not exist the way the physical body exists. It is not constantly present. It exists only when it is activated; otherwise, the "I" exists only as potential. Its very stability is only relative. It has various levels of activation, various levels of complexity, and various patterns of organization. It is constantly evolving. Nevertheless, it is that general feeling of familiarity, which is identified as the "I," that is experienced as though it is stable and unchanging. Moreover, since it exists now, and now is for the moment forever, it must have always existed. Furthermore, as it is usually an effective means of maintaining and enhancing the living organization, it aspires to exist forever, since that is the goal of life. This Reified I, which is a by-product of the increasing organization and integration of the central nervous system, is such a convenient abstraction that, for most people, it is its own reasons for being. However, this abstraction, which has evolved from the process of the increasing complexity and integration of the central nervous system, comes to have such an investment in its illusion of stability and continuity that the maintenance of the illusion may even impede the further integration of the human organization.

This reification of the I, this desire to maintain one's identity, begins to occur as consciousness becomes relatively more effective than ineffective in processing unfamiliar stimulation. As consciousness becomes more effective, there is an increase in the amount of positive affect associated with the general feeling of familiarity that typically accompanies consciousness. Therefore, the desire for this feeling of familiarity increases. During this early state of development, however, the Invested-Self is making relatively large changes with each shift in its complexity and integration. Therefore, the feeling of familiarity and the sense of identity of the individual is shifting and vague. The development of the self-concepts, however, begins to provide points of fixed reference within the Invested-Self. These points of fixed reference make the Invested-Self a more efficient tool for differentiating familiar from unfamiliar incoming stimulation. These points of fixed reference, however, are only abstractions of generalizations about reality. They are only representations of significant aspects of a variety of generalizations about reality, generalizations that are already less than precise representations of reality. These abstractions, which are the self-concepts, can be activated by a great range of experiences as though the experiences are all the same. In other words, self-concepts are more convenient ways of manipulating reality, but the abstract nature of self-concepts, which gives them their convenient illusion of stability also makes them resistive to change. A self-concept can encompass numerous generalizations about the self and the relationship of the self to reality, and it can encompass new generalizations and still be the same self-concept. For example, every time an experience occurs to activate my self-concept of myself as a psychologist, I can feel the reassuring familiarity associated with the self-concept. But, in reality, I am not the same psychologist I was a year ago. There may even be mounting evidence that the psychologist I am today is a far less effective psychologist than the psychologist I was a year ago. But when my self-as-psychologist self-concept is activated, I am reminded that I am still a psychologist, and that familiar self-concept reassures me and makes it unnecessary for me to attend to a certain amount of potentially disorganizing stimulation, information that I am aging, for instance, that might be inconsistent with my competent-psychologist self-concept.

In general, the development of self-concepts facilitates the reification of the I. Conflicts within the self do occur, however, that make the "I" experience less positive. When the feeling of familiarity comes to be associated with relatively dissimilar spheres of activity, and each of these spheres of activity develops into self-concepts, there is potential for conflict within these self-concepts. As a psychologist, I have developed the self-concept of being a helping-person. Yet, as a psychologist in the business of making a living, I may have developed the self-concept of a being a shrewd businessman. To a certain degree, shrewd businessmen take advantage of their clients. In taking advantage of one's clients, the shrewd businessman feels "familiarity" and positive affect. The psychologist, on the other hand, being a helper of others, does not take advantage of his counselees. If I operate within my self-concept as being a shrewd businessman, and I take advantage of my counselees/clients by encouraging them to remain counselees longer than is absolutely necessary, then my two self-concepts are in conflict. I may now feel "familiar" in operating under the activation of these two self-concepts, but I no longer feel as positive. In other words, the activation of my generalized self-concept, or Reified I, may be a familiar but unpleasant experience when I have conflict in self-concepts. I may attempt to cope with this unpleasant state of my Reified I through the use of psychological coping mechanisms, to repress the unpleasant affect. Or, more constructively, I may attempt to resolve the conflict between these two self-conflicts by further integrating the self so that there is the development of a higher order or even more general self-concept. For example, I might decide to retain only well-to-do counselees who have been given the choice to remain in therapy to refine their growth and then use the extra income to offset the lose of doing probono work. On the other hand, if I do not do something about the unpleasant state of my Reified I, in other words, if the conflict within my self-concepts continues over a period of time, I might be so unfortunate as to develop a negative self-concept. I might begin to conceive of myself as either a bad psychologist or a poor businessman. Then, in order to cope with this pervasive negative feeling that is activated within the Reified I, I might find it necessary to begin to suppress the Reified I, to suppress the feeling of familiarity, through the use of drugs or alcohol, or through the avoidance of the Self-Aware-Self by any method that reduces consciousness.

The Excessively Self-Contained Integrated-Self

This potential for the Reified I to facilitate the over use of psychological coping mechanisms or the development of negative self-concepts is a built-in liability of self-development. The Reified I, which may assist in the maintenance and further integration of organization, may also reverse the process of integration of the human organization. But even functioning as it evolved to function, the Reified I may keep the individual from evolving beyond the level of the Integrated-Self. To illustrate this subtle interference by the Reified I, we must further elaborate on the normal development of the Integrated-Self. In effective self-development, consciousness is efficient enough to allow and make desirable greater indulgence in the Self-Aware-Self. More time spent in the state of the Self-Aware-Self facilitates the development of numerous clearly articulated self-concepts, thereby, making the self even more efficient in maintenance and further integration of the organism. Development of higher-order self-concepts, such as professional ethics, value systems, or philosophies, and effective resolutions of the inevitable conflicts in self-concepts can create a more effective Integrated-Self. For example, if I develop the higher-order concept that a successful businessman/psychologist will only continue to be successful if he develops the reputation for helping his counselees more than he hurts them then I will realize that I can only feel good about myself as a businessman/psychologist if I help counselees more than I hurt them. Making my counselees dependent upon me so that I will make more money from them would be hurting them more than helping them. Therefore, I may be both a good psychologist and a shrewd businessman by enabling my counselees to gain independence from me, even though, in the process, I will not make more money from those counselees. In any case, my good reputation should bring in more counselees and more money in the long run.

As I continue to develop self-concepts that integrate my numerous lower-order self-concepts, in other words, as I continue to develop ethics, value systems, or a philosophy of life, I continue to develop a more integrated and functionally efficient and effective self. Since this further integration of the self is a positive experience, I am also making a further investment in the value of my Reified I. Those clearly articulated aspects of the Invested-Self, which are represented in the more integrated concepts of my Integrated-Self, are more readily available to the Self-Aware-Self and more capable of activating the feeling of "familiarity" that is the Reified I. Then the positive feeling of familiarity becomes increasingly identified with the uniqueness of the Integrated-Self.

For the Integrated-Self to continue the maintenance and further integration of the organization of the organism, however, the Integrated-Self must consist of abstractions of generalizations regarding reality that are changing to encompass the ever-changing environment. The Integrated-Self must consist of the stability associated with a relatively accurate representation of reality but have the flexibility to change with the continuously changing information about reality. In other words, the effective Integrated-Self must continually relate to external reality. The Reified I, on the other hand, is motivated by the desire to maintain familiarity, a familiarity that is activated by stability in the organization of the central nervous system. One way for the stability of the central nervous system to be facilitated is by focusing on the internal consistency of self-concepts to the relative exclusion of input from the external world. In other words, one way for the Integrated-Self to always have consistency with its values is to maintain an internal consistency of the central nervous system that will facilitate the comfortable feeling of familiarity desired by the Reified I. Moreover, this may be relatively easy to do in a well established Integrated-Self. Such a self has learned to deal effectively with reality, and has developed self-concepts that are generally consistent with reality. Therefore, such an Integrated-Self can continue to function effectively within the real world while primarily focusing on internal consistency.

This neatly, almost self-contained system, however, in excessively functioning in the service of the Reified I, has built in its own self-destruction. Such an Integrated-Self may become so efficient in serving the Reified I that the time required in such activity is relatively little—and the vast amount of time now available to the individual becomes an experience of meaninglessness.

Popular language usage suggests common knowledge of this problem. Terms such as "self-serving" and "self-centered" indicate that excessive concern with the self may ultimately be self-defeating. The self is an instrument that evolved as a more efficient way of maintaining and enhancing the organization of the human organism, and an efficiently functioning instrument serves its user better. But it is also possible to become so fascinated with an instrument that it becomes more important than the purpose for which the instrument was to be used.

For the most part, that which is good for the self is also good for the total human being. For the most part, further enhancement of the self, through further integration of the self, makes the self more effective in maintaining and enhancing the human organization. But excessive emphasis and concern with one aspect of the self may be deleterious for the total self and for the human organization. Hedonism, for example, is an emphasis on pleasurable limbic system feelings to the relative exclusion of the Cerebral-Self. Drug abuse is one illustration of excessive emphasis on the limbic-self. An even more extreme example might be the science fiction extrapolation from current research on direct brain stimulation. Certain areas of the limbic system, when directly stimulated by electrical current, are experienced as extremely pleasurable, and there is little cognition associated with this pleasure. Animals will continue self-inducing this direct brain stimulation until exhaustion and death. Science fiction writers have speculated that direct brain stimulation will be the illicit drug of the future.

It might also be assumed that there can be excessive emphasis on the Cerebral-Self, that people can think too much and feel too little. It is probably more accurate to say that some people emphasize the pleasurable feeling associated with mentation to the relative exclusion of the pleasurable feeling associated with more active use of the body. Therefore, the body suffers from inadequate use, and the total organization of the organism is undermined.

The Self-Aware-Self might also be overemphasized over the Functional-Self. In this case, not enough time is spent on attending to external stimulation, and conditions threatening to the total organization of organism may become unmanageable.

But the irony is that even the balanced emphasis on all aspects of the self, indicated by the development of the Integrated-Self, may also be self-defeating. As the self becomes more integrated and, therefore, generally more effective in maintaining the total organization of the organism, there is increasing pleasure associated with self-integration. One of the primary tools of self-integration is the central nervous system capacity to abstract, to represent complex external and internal events with simple cell assemblies. For the most part, the interaction of these abstractions is also more effective than the interaction of the larger cell assemblies that they represent. These abstractions are associated with limbic system affect; therefore, the activation of these abstractions is potentially pleasurable. The ultimate abstraction or representation of the self is the Reified I. The more integrated the self, the more effective the self has become in maintaining and enhancing the organization of the human organism, the more pleasure there is associated with activation of the Reified I. For the Integrated-Self, there is a danger that the Reified I will become the primary goal of the self and not just a point of reference for more efficient mentation. The self, in service of the Reified I, would seek to enhance its integration in the most efficient manner. Since the limbic system component of the Reified I is the feeling of familiarity, the self, in serving the Reified I, would seek to promote that feeling of familiarity by maintaining the integration of the components of the self to the exclusion of destructive non-self stimulation. Since the Integrated-Self is already quite efficient in handing most external stimulation, there would be relatively little immediate threat to the self from the external world. The eventual threat would be internal.

Although the slavish serving of the Reified I may seem to be the equivalent of electrical self-stimulation, this is an inaccurate analogy. The pleasure associated with the familiarity of the Reified I is not, in itself, strong enough to offset the anxiety associated with meaninglessness. The human organization is a dynamic organization. If it is not in the process of increasing its integration, it is disintegrating. Activity in the service of the Reified I is activity in the service of maintaining sameness. Such activity is not serving integration. Moreover, since the Integrated-Self is very efficient in merely maintaining its organization, the time required for organization maintenance activity is minimal. All that is left to the Integrated-Self, in service of the Reified I, is time spent in meaningless activity. Life that is not serving life has no reason to continue. The Integrated-Self, in the service of the Reified I, spends more and more of its time in the state of meaninglessness, besieged by anxiety associated with a threat from within, the anxiety of non-being. This is the "dark night of the soul," the attack that may come unexpectedly when it seems that the battle has been won. Now that all the needs have been sufficiently satisfied, and the body, though no longer young, is still strong, and the mind is filled with accumulated knowledge and apparent wisdom—suddenly there is the terrible moment of "so what?". This is the moment so poignantly expressed in the Peggy Lee song, "Is This All There Is?" The Integrated-Self that has fallen into the trap of excessively serving the Reified I may now ponder self-destruction as the only solution to the dilemma of the excessively self-contained self confronting the meaninglessness of itself.

The heroes in the classic fantasy novel, *The Worm Ouroboros*, confronted this same dilemma. After great trials they had vanquished all evil from the world. With the long awaited peace, came an unexpected emptiness. The heroes, whose reason for being was heroics, no longer had reason for being. In the last paragraph of the novel, the heroes rejoice as they witness the ancient evils reappearing magically into their world.

Unfortunately, we less than heroic human beings do not have to wish for the return of evil to our world. Glorious combat against evil is readily available for anyone who chooses the challenge. But there are other, perhaps less heroic ways of avoiding the potential trap of the Integrated-Self's excessively serving the Reified I. All of these are methods of transcending the self.

The Transcendent-Self

Self-transcendence is not the same thing as self-denial or selflessness, as in putting all others before oneself. Certainly self-transcendence is not the same thing as self-oblivion through excessive use of psychological coping mechanisms, drugs, chemicals, or suicide. To **transcend** *is to go beyond, and* **Self-transcendence** *means going beyond the narrow boundaries of the self that may be formed by the self-contained Integrated-Self.* "*Self-transcendence*" *means rising above the self-imposed limitations of the self-contained Integrated-Self by identification with that which is greater than the self. Therefore, self-transcendence is, in actuality, the creation of an even greater self,* **the Transcendent-Self.**

The Transcendent-Self is the final stage in the development of the self as an instrument for maintenance and further enhancement of the organization of the human organism. The Transcendent-Self rises above the potential limitations of the self-contained Integrated-Self. The Transcendent-Self avoids the anxiety and potential self-destructiveness of meaninglessness. The Transcendent-Self gives up some of the comforting familiarity of the Reified I for the challenging uncertainty and vitality of a limitless self.

Moments of self-transcendence may occur throughout the individual's life. It is even theoretically possible for a person to begin the transcendence of self while in the earlier stages of integrating the self, but this kind of self-transcendence is probably rare and would require considerable guidance. The natural way is to begin the development of the self-contained Integrated-Self and then to be goaded into self-transcendence by the anxiety of meaninglessness. So the creation of the Transcendent-Self is not likely to occur until the middle or later years.

Here is an example of the natural or usual process of self-transcendence. The individual has lived long enough to develop skills for efficiently and effectively satisfying the basic needs. That is, the person has to spend relatively little time and effort on the Internally and Externally Motivated Survival Needs, and the person has received sufficient love and esteem so as to be able to affirm the self through giving love and by behaving consistently according to self-determined values. The person may also have become proficient in actualizing his or her unique potentials. Now it is this very efficiency and effectiveness in need-gratification, in maintaining and affirming the self that makes available too much time, time that cannot be used to gratify needs that are already gratified. Therefore, most activity is likely to be meaningless activity. Now the person faces a crises-in-being—to continue biological life in a state of meaninglessness or non-being, to avoid the agonies of non-being by self-obliviation, or to face the anxiety of the unknown by giving up the comfortable familiarity of the Reified I through merging one's identity with the Transcendent-Self.

It might seem that self-transcendence would be the obvious choice. Maintaining life or, in other words, maintaining and enhancing the organization of the human organism has been given as the sovereign motivation of life. But not all people choose self-transcendence. The Edward Arlington Robinson poem, "Richard Cory," depicts this irony. Richard Cory was handsome and wealthy and admired by everyone, and "Richard Cory, one calm summer night, went home and put a bullet through his head." It seems a common experience for people to achieve a life-long goal of wealth or fame, only to discover that the achievement of their goal leaves them empty. Then, at the pinnacle of achievement, they begin to dissipate their lives.

Most people, however, are not so fortunate as to face this crisis-in-being at the pinnacle of achievement. In fact, most people may never face the crisis-in-being of self-transcendence. Most people spend their lives being only marginally effective and efficient in meeting the self-enhancement needs, or even the survival needs. From the point of view of our modern affluence, lives spend by most people around the world in the never-ending pursuit of survival might seem like wretched lives, but such lives are not meaningless. Grubbing in the cold earth for an edible root is very meaningful when one is near starvation. The irony is, people who live such arduous lives often report themselves to be more contented then those of us who have been protected from such deprivation by modern technology. Meaningfulness, however painful its attainment, is usually preferable to meaninglessness, however luxuriant.

There is an obvious logic related to the struggle to satisfy a deprived need that does not seem to hold for seeking self-transcendence. What deprived people must do to satisfy the survival needs might be difficult, but at least they usually know what they must do. They can derive a plan, however difficult it might be to execute, that will logically lead to the satisfaction of the survival needs. One can also derive a logical plan for the satisfaction of the self-affirmation needs. In choosing self-transcendence, however, logic does not reassure. What makes it difficult to choose self-transcendence is that there might be no apparent practical or even immediately conceivable plan to achieve the goals that must first be set if we are to begin the process of self-transcendence. By defining ones values so that they are within ones capacity to actualize, it is possible to behave consistently with those values and, thereby, achieve self-affirmation. For example, a psychologist may value honesty. Being consistent with that value, the psychologist may attempt to be accurate in everything said to a counselee.

In practicing such honesty, the psychologist can affirm him or herself. But if that same psychologist enters the diplomatic service, and serves in a conference with a potential enemy country on the issue of arms-reduction, the psychologist might find it more difficult to be "honest." In the former case, the psychologist has identified with the limited role of a psychologist. The self of the psychologist may encompass this role and, in behaving consistently with the values associated with that role, achieve self-integration. But for that psychologist to identify with the greater concerns of a whole nation, it is difficult to know what values to adopt and what behavior will in fact be consistent with those diverse values. In identifying with that which is greater than the boundaries of ones current self, self-integration and the comforting familiarity of the Reified I is difficult to maintain. Yet, if one retains the narrow boundaries of the self-contained self, in order to hold onto the Reified I, then the anxiety of meaninglessness might be inevitable.

Choosing a Transcendent Goal

In many ways identification with that which is greater than self might lead to self-destruction. That is part of the risk involved in self-transcendence. It is important to choose wisely that with which one is to identify. The general rule is, the goal of the Transcendent-Self should be one that promotes life. Conversely, to identify with a nation that has adopted a policy of wars of aggression is to identify with a goal and to attempt self-transcendence in the service of disorganization and death.

What transcendent goals serve life? This is the question that you must answer for yourself. The following discussion may guide your decision making, however.

Transcendent goals may vary from identification with one other person to identification with all of mankind. Transcendent goals may be a part of the physical world or of the abstract world that is created by our mentation. The transcendent goal may be only a small expansion beyond the current self, but it is more likely that a transcendent goal will greatly expand the boundaries of the self.

Our first experience with self-transcendence may occur when we give love. Being loved is not a transcending experience. It is self-affirming but it is the affirmation of having someone else confirm what we already wish to believe about ourselves. Neither is giving love to one's idealized loved-one an act of self-transcendence. This "giving of love" is merely another way of assuring one's self-affirmation by convincing ourselves that the love given by the other person is worth having. When you decide to give love to a real person you become concerned with *the actual* person. Therefore, you must expand your self to encompass that person's desirable as well as their not so desirable qualities. In giving love to an actual person, the self becomes more complicated and less integrated, but the activities necessary for the pursuit of reintegration of the self provide new sources of meaningfulness.

Giving love to one's children is also a potential experience of self-transcendence. As arduous as it may seem, giving love to infants and to small children, however, is usually not an act of self-transcendence. The parents of a small child are usually giving love to their conception of what they wish their child to be. In other words, they are merely affirming an aspect of their existing selves. It is only when the child matures and begins to become a separate person, and the parents transcend the narrow boundaries of their desired or idealized child, that the act of giving love, for example to a rebellious adolescent, becomes an act of self-transcendence.

Likewise, giving love to ones family might be merely an act of self-affirmation. What makes the giving of love an act of self-transcendence is giving love to a person or group of people as they actually exist rather than to an ideal of how they should be. Only by choosing the complexities of reality over the controlled simplicity of the ideal does one expand the boundaries of self and approach self-transcendence. The same principle that applies to giving love to one's family applies to giving loyalty to one's profession, company, race, religion, or nationality. To sacrifice yourself in the service of what you believe to be an ideal nation when that nation is bent on destroying all other nations is living, or perhaps even dying, within the narrow boundaries of self-illusion.

Self-transcendence through giving love may be all the self-transcendence that some people require to lead meaningful, fulfilling lives. For others, however, giving love may be only a stage in the process of self-transcendence. Or it may be the only experience in self-transcendence that a person achieves before descending into self-oblivion. The problem with giving love to individuals as a method of self-transcendence is that individuals might be too ephemeral. The person that you choose to love might change so drastically that you would not be serving life by continuing to love that person. For example, if the person you have chosen to love becomes self-destructive, you stand in too great a risk of having a part of your self destroyed if you continue to love that person. Furthermore, even a life-seeking person can die. Also, children grow up and physically and emotionally separate from their parents. With death and separation, the will to love may remain, but the capacity to fill one's time with activities that give to one's loved-ones is considerably lessened by the loved one's death or by separation from one's children. The departed-ones may continue to a part of your self, but they can no longer be meaningful transcendent goals that will provide meaningful activity.

Therefore, an effective transcendent goal usually must be greater than the love of individuals. An effective transcendent goal usually must be commitment to something greater than one's loved-one, one's children, and even one's family unit. In fact, the larger the number of people included in the unit to which you give your commitment the greater the probability that the unit will be an effective transcendent goal, providing you with meaningful activity. Of course, the larger the unit of people, the more complex the Transcendent-Self, and the more frustration one will encounter in attempting to achieve self-integration. This is the trade off you must make in transcending the narrow self-contained Integrated-Self. Existence will no longer be meaningless—but neither will it be easy.

Therefore, effective transcendent goals are likely to be abstractions, commitment to which may *indirectly* benefit other human beings. The following are examples of transcendent goals that are likely to lead to the creation of a Transcendent-Self and, therefore, to promote meaningful and fulfilling lives: national unity in the service of national and international peace; environmental conservation; pure science or the application of pure science to promote rather than to destroy life; the clarification and expansion of knowledge about human behavior; the creation of esthetic experiences that may contribute to refinement in the integration of the human organization; and the creation and expression of philosophical and theological principles and systems to guide the further integration within individual human organizations and the integration of individuals with other individuals.

These transcendent goals are unlikely to be achievable within the lifetime of one individual. In fact, they might never be achieved. It is this difficulty or impossibility of achievement that makes a transcendent goal effective in promoting meaningfulness throughout the remaining life of an individual. On the other hand, the lure of such a powerful source of meaningfulness might mislead some individuals. We are all faced with the inevitable meaninglessness that occurs after mastery of the skills for satisfying one of the lower-order needs. There are those who, when then confronted with a difficulty in satisfying the next level of need, will attempt to prematurely adopt one of these transcendent goals. For example, young people often get involved in great causes, when their actual motivation is identification with that cause so that the glory associated with the cause will provide them with the self-affirmation they are not yet able to provide for themselves. Therefore, their purpose is self-affirmation and not the achievement of the transcendent goal. Considering the difficulty of achieving a transcendent goal, it is unlikely that the young person will achieve his or her personal goal of self-affirmation through identification with a transcendent goal. The premature adoptions of a transcendent goal might only lead to frustration, disillusionment, and embitterment.

Effective self-transcendence is not likely to occur until the person has first been effective in satisfying the four basic needs. If self-transcendence is to serve the sovereign motivation of maintenance and further integration of the organization the human organism, it must proceed from the integration of the self. If life is to go beyond the level of integration imposed by *human* life, the life-promoting instrument that is the self must first be developed to its ultimate, and then transcended. The form of life that may yet be achieved through the integration of the many transcendent units of mankind is only now in the process of evolving. *The evolution of life-beyond-human-life depends on how many of us have the courage to transcend the narrow boundaries of our individual identities to join with each other to create the next level beyond the Transcendent-Self*—**the Integrated-Transcendent-Self.**

Applying the Theory

How the Helper Should Help

Speculation on How the Self Should Work

I have attempted to create a way of understanding how and why the self developed. Having this understanding, or at least the illusion of such understanding, I now feel better able to understand why and how I should be helping those who come to me for psychological counseling.

Let me emphasize the obvious. This book has been primarily an exercise in speculation. I began by making assumptions about the nature of life, and I will end by making assumptions about effective ways of enhancing life's most complex expression, the human self. Probably the most speculative assumption that I made is about the nature and function of consciousness. The definition given for this term provides the means for understanding the further development and integration of the self as well as suggestions for overcoming obstacles to that development.

For the most part, I have limited myself to this relatively modest objective. This book is intended as theory, as an attempt to conceptualize order out of seeming chaos, not as a compilation of facts. If I had sufficient facts about self-development, I wouldn't need theory. Yes, my responsibility in creating a useful theory is to be consistent with known facts, but it is primarily to be logical in extrapolating from those facts. The facts that have been generally established by replicatable research are still at the conceptual level of the interactions within single neurons or simple cell assemblies. I have made psychological extrapolations well beyond Sommerhoff's careful and precise neurological extrapolations from these known neural interactions. Sommerhoff demonstrated that, from what we do know about neurons, we can use logic to design models of more complex cell assemblies that could account for such higher mental functions as imagery and memory. He does not say that his models are the way the brain actually functions, only that we could account for these mental activities if the brain does follow his models. Building on Sommerhoff's work, I say that even more complex neurophysiology could also account for consciousness and other levels of self-development. Then, based upon known neurological facts, and neurological speculation, my speculation at the psychological levels of conceptualization should have firmer foundation.

The key to understanding and accepting this theory is understanding and accepting consciousness as a real and useful experiences and not just an epiphenomenon. I don't know that my argument for the existence of consciousness has convinced you. If not, I believe that the definition of consciousness I've given will at least serve as an operational definition that will further explain why consciousness as defined makes consciousness a necessary goal of psychotherapy. Explaining that necessity is the goal of this application section of the book.

Again, this is all speculation, but I hope useful speculation. Since this book is just speculation, I apologize for the didactic tone that I have often taken. I probably needed that tone to assure myself that I was on the right track so that I would have the courage to continue speculating. So forgive me as I continue in that tone.

Restating the Theory of Self-Development

You recall, I suggested that a useful theory, in addition to being supported by facts and having internal consistency, must also have application. Let me begin this section on applying the theory by reiterating (and perhaps reifying) my theoretical explanation for the progression from non-life and simple life to higher consciousness.

Life is an unstable organization of otherwise nonliving matter that tends to maintain its organization through increasing the integration of its organization. The human central nervous system is the most integrated form of living matter that has yet evolved on Earth. But the human organism can continue to evolve, can continue to increase the integration of its central nervous system through levels of increasing integration of the self.

The self *is a series of levels of integration of the human central nervous system that enables human beings to more effectively maintain and enhance their intracellular and intercellular organizations.* **The function of the self** *is to coordinate the interaction between any event that might disorganize the person's central nervous system organization and the behavior that might have a corrective effect upon the disorganizing event.* The lowest level of self, **The Limbic-Self,** is the loci of the cell assemblies that motivate the human being to act. **The Cerebral-Self** is the location of all the information that ultimately enables human beings to predict the consequences of their behavior. The level of central nervous system integration labeled **The Invested-Self** is the storehouse of all the information in the Cerebral-Self that also activates the limbic system feeling of belongingness. **The Functional-Self** level of integration of the central nervous system is also called consciousness. **Consciousness** *is that moment of synthesis between activation of a cell assembly in the Cerebral-Self, or in the Invested-Self, and the feeling of recognition and associated feelings activated in the Limbic-Self.* Consciousness functions to free the cerebrum from limiting activation of limbic system arousal and focusing so as to make possible the activation of other generally similar cell assemblies in the cerebrum. *This sequential activation of cerebral cell assemblies facilitated by consciousness is called* **Sequential Mentation,** *the most integrated form of which is thinking.* When cell assemblies of the

Invested-Self are activated by consciousness, the human being is functioning at the integrational level of **The Self-Aware-Self.** Through this self-focusing process, aspects of the Self-Aware-Self are synthesized into self-concepts, and more specifically into that which we generally think of as the self, **The Self-Concepts-Self.** When self-concepts are clearly articulated and conflicts between self-concepts within the Self-Concepts-Self are generally resolved, the individual is functioning at the level of **The Integrated-Self.**

Once the Limbic-Self has begun to generate feelings, feeling become motivation for the continued development of the self. As the self develops to the Self-Aware-Self, the maintenance and enhancement of the self becomes it own motivation. Eventually, mentation and specifically language becomes the most efficient motivator.

The Four Basic Human Needs Human beings functioning at the level of the Integrated-Self have developed the skills for satisfying the four basic human needs: **1.Internally Motivated Survival Needs, 2. Externally Motivated Survival Needs, 3. Externally Satisfied Self-Enhancement Needs,** and **4. Internally Satisfied Self-Enhancement Needs.** Such individuals are skillful enough to satisfy these needs with relatively little effort. They take care of themselves physically, and they place a high value on their selves. As such, Integrated-Selves are highly efficient and effective at satisfying the sovereign motivation of life, the maintenance and enhancement of the living organization.

The Transcendent-Self. But the particular integrational evolution of the central nervous system that led to the development of the Integrated-Self is not without built-in design problems. Self-integration can also be self-defeating. The *excessively* self-contained Integrated-Self may come to derive so much satisfaction from mentation that affirms the experience of being consistent, and become so efficient at this process, that relatively little time is required to maintain self-consistency. Therefore, the excessively self-contained Integrated-Self spends more and more time in a state of meaninglessness, or a state in which too little activity is devoted to the satisfaction of needs because these needs are already satisfied. The anxiety associated with this state of meaninglessness either drives the excessively self-contained Integrated-Self into oblivion-seeking or it goads that self into the next level of human integration, the Transcendent-Self. **Self-Transcendence** *is identification of the self with that which is greater than the self.* Through striving for a transcendent-goal, a goal that is so unachievable as to be unattainable in the life of the individual, the Transcendent-Self has enough challenge to escape from meaninglessness. The formerly self-contained Integrated-Self is no longer integrated; the complexity of the Transcendent-Self is such that self-contained integration is impossible. Therefore, motivation toward integration is restored, and the individual is continually in a state of need-deprivation requiring meaningful activity. The Transcendent-Self, though less integrated than the Integrated-Self, has greater potential for maintaining the self, since there is far less risk of meaninglessness.

After consciousness and the Functional-Self have developed, freewill becomes possible, and this also means that responsibility and irresponsibility are possible.

Finally, the theory is applied to explain how irresponsible behavior, meaning behaving in ways that are counter to maintenance and enhancement of the living organization, leads to the development of ineffective psychological coping mechanisms and negative self-concepts.

The Effective Use of Consciousness

The person who makes effective use of consciousness to maintain and enhance the self does not need psychotherapy. Others who are not so fortunate can use psychotherapeutic help in learning or restoring their effective use of consciousness. But what is this "effective use of consciousness" that psychotherapy intends to teach or restore? Consciousness or the Functional-Self is a self-process that makes available a greater number of cerebral cell assemblies. When more such cell assemblies are activated, the possibility increases that mentation or actions will occur that will eventually solve problems. **The effective use of consciousness** *is any use of consciousness that facilitates problem-solving and thereby enables the person to obtain or recover a more functional level of neurological organization so as to further enhance the integrational level of that person's central nervous system.*

You will recall, however, that the Functional-Self or consciousness is not the most frequently occurring level of self-integration. Most threats or demands upon the human being are handled automatically. When there is no automatic mechanism for handling a demand, consciousness may be employed. Consciousness is also more likely to occur in those individuals who have a positive history with consciousness.

This is the process for the *non*-psychopathological person, one who has a positive history with consciousness. In such fortunate people, even intense arousal is often experienced as positive, since in the past such arousal states have eventuated in problem-solving. As with anyone, when a threat occurs the central nervous system is to some degree disorganized. This leads to some degree of arousal, perhaps even intense arousal. Consciousness then operates to make available more of the Cerebral-Self for solving the problem that is creating the threat. In these individuals, even when a solution is not readily forthcoming, the habit of enduring delayed gratification enables the individual to tolerate the anxiety that begins to accompany this period of cerebral disorganization. With this capacity to tolerate anxiety, with the expectation that delayed gratification will eventual lead to problem-solving, consciousness continues, and problem-solving is more likely to occur.

Things Go Wrong

Most people probably do have positive experiences with consciousness. Unfortunately, there are still a considerable number of people do not have enough such positive experiences. The thing that goes wrong with these people is what metal health professionals term psychopathology.

In terminology used previously, psychopathology may be thought of as "irresponsible" behavior. **Psychopathology** *is a condition in which individuals are impeded, in their desire to maintain and enhance their organization, by defective neuroanatomy or physiology or by ineffective processes for handling disruptive stimuli impinging upon the central nervous system.* These ineffective processes are all the result of the inability or the failure to use consciousness, or the inappropriate use of consciousness. The inappropriate use of consciousness can result in the misuse of psychological coping mechanisms, in negative self-concepts, or in the excessively self-contained Integrated-Self.

For the *psychopathic* individual, here is **the typical sequence of psychopathological psychoneurological events**, or events that occur when there is disruption in the neurological organization of the human being and the stimulus causing that disruption is not handled automatically. When the unfamiliar stimulus impinges upon the central nervous system, the central nervous system is to some degree disorganized. A component of the limbic system is activated to instigate a general arousal of the Cerebral-Self, and more of the cerebral cortex is activated. On the psychological level this arousal might be experienced on a continuum from alertness, through excitement, to being a bit on edge, and then to becoming irritated, eventually angered, and then enraged. Arousal at all levels of intensity motivates the person to seek out and if possible to focus on the source of the disruption. But high levels of arousal are themselves disruptive to the cerebral organization. If intense arousal does not eventuate in problem-solving within a reasonable amount of time, the degree of disruption in the cerebral organization activates limbic system feelings of anxiety and then desperation.

The Helper's Task

The idealized course of self-development, from the relatively uninte-grated infant-self to the highly complex integrated level of the Transcendent-Self, is the exception and not the rule. Most of us have stumbled and stalled in our journey along this developmental pathway. As I see it, **the psychological counselor's task** *is to help the individual analyze where and why this stumbling has occurred and then to assist the individual to design strategies for continuing the struggle to achieve more effective self-integration.*

Neurophysiologically, the organism is motivated to maintain and enhance its organization. Psychologically speaking, this means that human beings want to feel good. They want to avoid or to escape from the anxiety that accompanies physical disorders or psychological insta-bility, and they want the pleasurable feelings associated with using their bodies as they were intended to be used and enhancing their self-esteem through integrative mentation, such as self-affirming thoughts. So, before teaching the effective use of consciousness, typically the psycho-logical helper intervenes to reduce disruptive emotions so that con-sciousness will more readily occur. Then the psychological helper teaches the counselee more successful coping habits that will reinforce the habit of consciousness and make effective consciousness a more likely occurrence for the counselee.

Effective Consciousness Means Consciousness of Feelings

The subtitle of this book, "Effective Consciousness as the Goal of Psychotherapy" seems to indicate that thought or cognitive processes are what are most valued in the therapeutic process. After all, most peo-ple think of being conscious as having thoughts. But, as I have sug-gested, in helping people, awareness and management of feelings is primary. Logic and cognitions are but tools to achieve what is far more important for most people positive feelings. **Feelings** *guide a person to more effective use of self-maintaining and self-enhancing actions but more important, feelings give reason for being.* Feelings are the cues that alert us to threats to the self but feelings are what direct us toward actions that give joy. Without feelings we might fail to survive but without feelings we would also have no reason to survive. I have said that once life has by chance been initiated, our progress as a species from inorganic to organic life all the way through most of the levels of self-development is inevitable. This could be taken to mean that because of this inevitability, this seeming predetermination, we are no more than robots guided by survival and growth software but we are not robots. Once, also by chance, when we organic being had developed a limbic system and feelings, the limbic system positive feelings gave us motivation to seek more of those feeling, so that eventually experiencing those feelings became the prime motivation for continuing to be. It is unlikely that we will develop robots with limbic systems. Why bother? It would only further complicate an already complicated machine, and perhaps make robots frighteningly human-like. In spite of the pursuit of feelings by Data, of Star Trek fame, robots of the future will undoubtedly be programmed to survive but they probably won't have any feelings about it.

But as you well know, for non-robotic humans, feelings are not all positive. Often there is more pain than pleasure. It is the need to establish an acceptable balance between the positive and negative feelings inevitably encountered in living that makes effective consciousness a necessity. As long as we continue to experience relatively more positive than negative feelings we will probably be willing to endure our share of negative feelings and go on struggling to live.

The Challenge and Who Should Help

There are many things that might impede self- integration. At the most basic level, there is the hereditary absence of the anatomical components necessary to bring about effective integration. The physician might be the recommended helper when self-integration is impeded by an anatomical inadequacy. But even in such cases, anatomical deficiency is seldom the exclusive problem. Psychological helpers are needed to assist these anatomically deficient people in their attempts to compensate for those deficiencies.

Most people who come to Clinical Psychologists, Psychiatrists, Social Workers, Counselors, and other psychological helpers, however, are basically anatomically complete and functioning as Self-Aware-Selves and beyond. The challenge for counselees functioning ineffectively at the higher levels of self-development is to use effective consciousness to become aware of and manage feelings. Feelings below the level of awareness, and not available to conscious management, tend too often to mismanage the person. In other words, if you don't manage your feelings they might mismanage you.

The challenge for the psychological helper is to enable the counselee to become aware of disruptive feelings, even when awareness of many of those feelings will initially cause even greater disruption. The first step in that therapeutic process is usually providing labels for the feelings that are causing the disruption. Labeling the feelings through more effective use of consciousness gives one the power over those disruptive feelings. *If I know what to call it, perhaps I can learn what to do about it.* If I know that I am feeling *self-doubt* rather than *indignation* when I am criticized, I can ask the criticizer to give me more information before I angrily defend myself. Who know? Maybe he's right, and I should thank him rather than argue with him. Even if he's not right, even if he's just a jerk, then I've given myself time to calm down and manage my emotions so that I won't then waste my time arguing with someone who is not worth the effort.

What to Call the Helper and the Helpee?

For people whose problem is not primarily physical, the help needed is, for want of a better term, **psychological,** *by which I mean an understanding of ones thoughts, feelings, and behavior.* Therefore, the helper needed is one trained in understanding how people can be helped to more effectively think, manage their feelings, and behave. The formal training of such helpers is in Clinical Psychology, Psychiatry, Psychiatric Social Work, Psychiatric Nursing, and Psychological Counseling. The skills needed by practitioners of all of these disciplines are methods for imparting all the skills of living. So what should we call this omniscient omnipotent helper? Unreal, of course. But let's give the real and more modest practitioner who attempts this difficult task some title general enough to cover most of the needed skills. Some of the time I will use the terms psychotherapist and psychological counselor, but most of the time I will use the more generic term, psychological helper. And what to call the person receiving this help? Since the terms helpee and therapee are absurd, and the term patient is too narrow, I'll use the term, counselee.

However, *the first task of the psychological helper is the assessment of the relative importance of any anatomical or physiological problems.* Where such problems are a significant impediment, and there exists the possibility these difficulties can be rectified, referral to the appropriate physician is the first responsibility of the psychological helper. To put it another way, in our zeal to help with our psychological skills, we must never forget the integration we wish to enhance psychologically begins with physical integration.

Psychopathology in General

Psychopathology *is any central nervous system impairment or any behavior that disrupts the living organization or impedes its further integration.* **Psychopathological Behavior** *is any behavior that has as its primary goal the immediate reduction of anxiety but in a manner that reduces the effectiveness of consciousness and diverts consciousness from solving the problem that is causing the anxiety.* **The process of overcoming psychopathology** *is the restoration of that which psychopathology most immediately impairs—consciousness.* The ultimate solution to psychopathological avoidance of anxiety-producing problems is more effective use of consciousness.

I have already said that psychotherapy is not purely or even primarily a logical process. Logic is affect free; therefore, no human being can be purely logical. Remember, according to this theory, consciousness is a synthesis between the Cerebral-Self and the Limbic-Self. Consciousness is being avoided in psychopathological behavior because the affective components of consciousness in the person with the habit of psychopathology is too contaminated with negative affect. In such people, the feelings associated with being conscious are painful, and it is difficult to endure that pain long enough to solve the problem causing the painful affect. Therefore, the process of psychotherapy is one of gradually encouraging greater use of consciousness, while at the same time enabling the counselee to control the potentially overwhelming negative affect through the use of other psychotherapeutic aids.

Psychotropic medication is of course one such aid, the intention of which is a chemical disruption of the synapses transmitting the negative affect from the limbic system to the cortex. When anxiety is otherwise uncontrollable, psychotropic medication may be indicated. But one side effect of such medication is often to reduce motivation to attack the cause of the anxiety. A less debilitating technique for managing anxiety would be some form of positive self-process, such as self-suspension (e.g. meditation) or non-cerebral activation of positive limbic system states (e.g. exercise). Through these direct methods of manipulating the body, with their indirect calming effect upon the limbic system, a condition of positive affect is restored that can then interact with the Cerebral-Self to allow relatively less painful consciousness. In this state, the Functional-Self can proceed to problem-solve. An example of this essential technique will be given in the model session later in this book.

Helping Behavior of the Psychological Helper

Bearing in mind all of these theory-based general recommendations, what does the psychological helper actually do to help counselees? What follows is neither a compendium of psychotherapies nor a detailed description of an exotic new therapy. Rather, based upon this theory of consciousness and human development, the remainder of this chapter and the two subsequent chapters will offer generalizations about who needs what kind of help. This will be followed by a model of *how* this might be done.

The general answer is, of course, the psychological helper does anything that he or she can do to improve or restore the counselee's effective use of consciousness. Practically speaking, this means starting with the counselee at whatever level of self-integration is currently possible for that person. One doesn't expect *immediate* problem-solving from an anxiety-ridden counselee. On the other hand, for the psychotherapist to begin to be effective, the counselee must of course be conscious enough to interact with the therapist. The level of central nervous system integration, or consciousness, operating in the intoxicated or the hallucinatory counselee makes such counselees unavailable for psychotherapy. Yes, intoxication and hallucination are relative states of course, and even the psychotropic medicated state is a degree of intoxication. So some psychotherapeutic intervention *can* be attempted with counselees in these states. But for effective psychotherapy to take place, it is probably best to wait until such counselees are functioning a higher level of consciousness.

After determining that the counselee is adequately conscious, the next task is the establishment of a climate of trust. In establishing trust one must be more of an artist than a technician. But the essence of the process is openness and accuracy of information exchange. The psychological helper must self-disclose so as to reduce the likelihood that fearful counselees will misinterpret the unknowns in the therapeutic situation and react to them as threats. This means that the psychological helper must share both feelings and thoughts in describing the psychotherapeutic process and in reacting to the counselee's beginning description and explanation of the problem. This also means that in the initial stages of psychotherapy, the psychological helper might occasionally be more active than the counselee. The psychotherapeutic skill required is that of being sensitive to when the counselee's level of comfort can allow the psychotherapist to become less active. If it is evident that anxiety is too great to allow the emergence of effective counselee-consciousness, the psychological helper should become very directive in recommending the necessary psychotherapeutic interventions to enable the counselee to manage anxiety. This intervention may be accomplished relatively rapidly, as in the use of reassurance or relaxation techniques, or it may require numerous training sessions before the counselee is ready to attempt to become more effective in the use of consciousness.

After the counselee begins to think along with the psychological helper, the helper's role shifts to that of consultant. The psychological helper then begins to interact with the counselee in those ways that will bring to the counselee's consciousness the awareness of the psychopathological habits. In other words, some degree gentle confrontation must begin to occur. Counselees will be directed to identify disruptive feelings and then to recognize the psychological coping mechanisms that they have habitually used to control those feelings.

The purpose of identifying and exploring the function of the psychopathological behavior is to lead the counselee to consider the adaptation of more effective behavior. At this point in the process of psychotherapy, it is assumed that anxiety is managed enough that consciousness is a tolerable process. The counselee can now see beyond the necessity of enduring a period of further discomfort to that time when the adaptation of more effective behaviors will solve the problem causing the anxiety. At this point in psychotherapy, the psychological helper again becomes directive. Strategies are recommended and encouraged that will enable the counselee to continue problem-solving outside of the psychotherapeutic sessions. The psychological helper now functions almost as a coach, giving feedback in subsequent sessions on the effectiveness of the counselee's problem-solving strategies so that the counselee can attempt to go forth and be even more effective.

But not all psychotherapy goes this well. The counselee may not choose to change.

There is one absolute in the helping relationship. *Whether or not the psychological helper respects the counselee's decision, the psychological helper must respect the counselee's right to decide.* This also means that the counselee has the right to choose psychopathology. Only the counselee knows if the anxiety is bearable or unbearable. Only the counselee can know if it is necessary to escape the anxiety through continuing the psychopathological avoidance of problem-solving. **The psychological helper's responsibility** *is to accurately disclose his or her thoughts and feelings in response to the counselee's seemingly dysfunctional behavior and to explore possible harmful consequences of the continuation of that behavior.* But only the counselee can decide if the consequences are preferable to enduring the anxiety of change.

As risky as this principle might seem, its intended consequence is the ultimate affirmation of the counselee. The important message is, the psychological helper believes that the counselee is ultimately responsible whether or not he or she seems to be behaving that way. **The psycholog-**

ical helper is saying, *"I believe that, given the intensity of your feelings, you are doing the best that you can do. But I also believe that I shouldn't do for you what you must eventually do for yourself. I will work with you because I believe that together we can find a way for you to more effectively care for yourself."*

This general outline of the psychotherapeutic process is of course descriptive of many if not most of the types of psychotherapy. By following this general outline, however, it may be possible for the psychotherapist to avoid the pitfalls of excessive emphasis on one or more aspect of a particular psychotherapeutic process. In other words, this theory of psychotherapy recommends that psychotherapy is more than just exploring the unconscious, achieving insight, overcoming resistance, analyzing transference, arranging reinforcement schedules, or even focusing on the effective use of consciousness. Effective psychotherapy is doing *whatever* is necessary to eventually restore the counselee's effective use of consciousness. At any given time in the psychotherapeutic process, most any psychotherapeutic technique might be applicable.

The relative emphasis that the psychological helper places on managing affect versus developing cognitive skills is dictated by the degree of pervasiveness of the counselees' psychopathological inability to use consciousness or by their avoidance of consciousness. In the neurologically intact counselee whose intelligence is adequate, only a minimal amount of the psychological helper's initial efforts may need to be spent on facilitating skills for managing the emotions. Once disruptive emotions are brought under control and the counselee begins to feel comfortable using consciousness, most of these intact counselees already have most of the cognitive skill they will need to solve problems.

The specific strategies used by psychological helpers to increase the effectiveness of consciousness are so varied as to make it necessary for the psychological helper to be a Jack-of-all-trades. The general discipline that is concerned with improving the effectiveness of consciousness, from which psychological helpers borrow, is of course the discipline of Education. All academic disciplines attempt to add information to the Cerebral Self that can be used in problem-solving. Some of these academic disciplines focus more specifically on the process of thinking, one of the effective uses of consciousness. These are the study of philosophy, logic, semantics, learning theory, and effective spoken and written use of language. One of the most useful problem-solving strategies comes from the scientific disciplines, the scientific method. Therefore, to facilitate the counselee's more effective use of consciousness, psychological helpers need to have at least rudimentary skills in all of these disciplines. *But the specialized skill and talent that psychological helpers must bring to the challenge of facilitating the counselee's effective use of consciousness is expertise in understanding and managing feelings.* Psychological helpers must begin the process of assisting their counselees by freeing these counselees from the debilitating grip of anxiety or the disrupting rush of anger before guiding them into developing cognitive skills.

The Ineffective Behaviors

Character Disorders

The person who has developed effective use of consciousness usually solves problems before extremes of arousal are reached. The psychopathological individual also attempts to avoid extremes, but not through problem-solving. Rather, since consciousness has been ineffectively used in the past, immediate action or psychological coping mechanisms are used instead to moderate arousal long before it reaches the intensity of anxiety.

In some psychopathological individuals, even the mid range of arousal will be avoided. When aroused to the level of anger, or perhaps only to the level of intense interest, these people who have been chronically ineffective in solving problems come to associate these degrees of arousal with the anxiety that occurred in these circumstances in the past. Disorganizing stimuli that might be experience by others as challenging are experienced by such individuals as threatening, and these psychopathological individuals retreat behind psychological coping mechanisms, and subsequently solve fewer and fewer problems. Therefore, few effective coping habits are developed, and the external world becomes more and more threatening.

These ineffective individual have been labeled Character Disorders. They have developed such habits as excessive dependency, learned helpless depression, passive-aggressive manipulation, and a variety of other interpersonal manipulative skills to seduce others into caring for them so they won't have to care for themselves.

The essential task of the psychological help in working with Character Disorders is to avoid being one of those "others." In the face of all the manipulative pleading and anger, the answer to "Do it for me." is "No." This gentle and persistent no, in spite of all the counselee's pleading or protests is the most caring thing the psychological helper can do.

While this refusal to be manipulated is taking place, the helper must also be doing whatever is possible to nevertheless reduce the counselee's anxiety. In addition to persistently recommending direct anxiety reducing strategies, perhaps the most effective anxiety reducing strategy are recommendations that reflect the counselor's unswerving belief that the counselee can eventually become self-sufficient. This faith is manifested by unflappable patience and even a modicum of humor in the face of the counselee's frequently absurd behavior. With patience, it is believed that the counselee will eventually tire of eternal avoidance and begin the effective use of consciousness.

The Psychopath

There is another psychopathological individual who at times *seems* to be as effective as the non-psychopathological person in managing intense arousal states. These are the psychopaths. In states of intense arousal, these people have usually been able to effect changes in disruptive stimuli and, as a result, have reinforced their use of actions that have been motivated by intense arousal. But the changes made in the disruptive stimuli, under the impetus of intense arousal, are too often only temporary. The temporary suppression of an external threat is an illusion of problem-solving. The threatening agents (usually people) are often themselves active agents seeking to solve their own problems. These agents find other ways to threaten the psychopathic individual. In interpersonal or social interactions, this often means the psychopath's aggressive behavior stimulates counter-aggression. These intense-arousal-action people obtain

immediate gratification at the expense of incurring even greater long-term problems.

Is psychopathic behavior the result of genetic or organic impairment or is it learned? We don't yet know. The underlying psychodynamic seems to be the inability to identify and feel for others. Their resorting to immediate gratification, to reduce their anxiety, often harms others, and this eventually fails to manage the anxiety because the others retaliate. So, whatever is the cause of their behavior, they are functioning a lower, ineffective level of self-organization. Treatment will mean whatever it takes to enable them to become more effective in the use of consciousness to develop a more effective level of self-organization.

Psychopaths, with their habit of seeking immediate gratification through action motivated by intense arousal do not usually develop effective use of consciousness. Typically, consciousness is not required to coordinate aggressive action, so action impulsive individuals do not develop effective consciousness. The effective use of consciousness requires the habit of **delaying gratification,** which is not something the psychopath is inclined to do.

So, the psychopath must be helped to delay gratification. But how to do that when the psychopath's immediate gratification is so over-learned? Pure logic can be used here. The psychopath, like all immature individuals, is extremely self-centered. So use logic to appeal to the psychopath's self-centeredness. Become the agent of the psychopathic counselee, an agent who job is to suggest short-term strategies this *will* give immediate gratification, so as to enable management of the counselee's anxiety until long-term cumulative gains begin to be experienced and the counselee begins to believe that delayed gratification will pay off.

It might be useful to differentiate psychopaths from sociopaths. Unlike psychopaths, sociopaths do identify with and feel for others. The others, however, are limited to members of a narrow segment of society, e.g. as in the Mafia family. Members of the larger society do not engender caring feelings in sociopaths, and they are treated by sociopaths as objects rather than people. After all, "It's just business."

Of course, the helper in working with psychopaths or sociopaths must also be logical. Learning to delay gratification is learning to be mature. For a person who has reached adulthood without becoming psychologically of societally mature, there will be no instant maturation. It is only logical to expect psychotherapy with the psychopath or sociopaths to be difficult and long-term, and these counselees must choice to remain in therapy. But always remember, it *is* the counselee's choice (*even* when the psychopath or sociopath is referred by the court).

Psychosis

Another group of counselees also need patient and long-term care. This is the severest form of psychopathology, the psychosis. The psychoses are generally classified as physiogenic or psychogenic, or as organic or functional. It has typically been assumed that when there is psychotic behavior in an individual with recognizable damage to the central nervous system (trauma or disease) that the psychosis has been caused by the neurophysiological damage. Therefore, the treatment of choice for such counselees is medication and perhaps custodial care. Psychological counseling is also recommended, primarily to assist the afflicted individual to compensate for the incapacity. When psychotic behavior has been observed, and there is no apparent neurological impairment, it was assumed that the psychotic behavior was primarily functional or learned behavior. For these counselees, some form of psychotherapy other than compensatory might have been recommended. New studies, however, primarily those using identical twins who have been raised apart, suggest that almost *all* psychotic behavior has an underlying physical basic. It is perhaps more accurate to say that in psychotic individuals the capacity of the central nervous system to achieve effective integration is less than it needs to be. This hereditarily or traumatically acquired ineffective of the central nervous system makes it more likely that such individuals will fail to develop effective uses of consciousness.

The other dichotomy in psychoses is schizophrenic vs. affective, in which schizophrenic psychosis is primarily a thought-disorder and affective psychosis is an extreme mood disturbance. Organic deficiency is probably a determining factor in both of these forms of psychosis. In the schizophrenic, there is probably impairment in the cerebrum. In the affective psychoses, however, the organic defect might be in the limbic system or in the interaction between the limbic system and the cerebrum, causing the counselee to be grossly ineffective in managing emotions. The observed behavior is mood swings accompanied by thought disorder, or in other words, ineffective use of consciousness.

Therefore, understanding psychotic behavior, whether schizophrenic or affective, organic or functional, begins with understanding the function of the counselee's genetically or traumatically determined neurophysiology. But, given their underlying neurophysiological conditions, individual counselees must still attempt to cope with life's challenges. The resulting learned behaviors, the ineffective coping habits, are what is observed and labeled as psychotic. Therefore, psychosis is "caused" by genetics or trauma *and* by experience.

Based on this assumption, the treatment of choice for all psychotic counselees is both medical and psychological. The medical treatment is the minimum amount of medication needed to compensate for the physiological ineffective or, when the specific biochemical deficiency is unknown, the minimum amount of general central system depressant to keep the anxiety from overwhelming the individual. The "minimum" is stressed because as has been stated the one typical side-effect of psychotropic medication is interference with the body's natural method of continuing self-integration and managing anxiety, that is, the use of consciousness.

The non medical role of the psychological helper with the psychotic counselee is three fold: using emotional support or milieu therapy to reduce disrupting threats to the individual, and teaching the patient to use compensatory techniques for managing anxiety. Then, the role of the psychological helper with the psychotic is the same as with all other counselees, the use of counseling and psychotherapy to make more efficient the counselee's use of consciousness.

The definition of the term "psychosis" is problematic. Typically, psychotic behavior is described as a distortion in the patient's perception of reality that manifests itself in hallucinatory or delusional thinking. I would prefer to define **psychosis** *as an inability to reason logically that has resulted in a person's inability to care for him or herself* **or** *in some expression of that reasoning process that others find too deviant to tolerate.* In other words, we label people psychotic if they are unable to care for themselves or if their ways of caring for themselves so disturb us that wish to have them removed from our presence. This explanation suggests that although the underlying cause of psychosis, with or without obvious neurophysiological impairment, is ineffective use of consciousness, whether people who are ineffective in their use of consciousness are labeled as psychotic is also a function of how they affect other people. Some individuals who have gross defects in the use consciousness are inoffensive to others and are therefore considered cranks or at worst "ambulatory" psychotics. Others, who are far less defective in their use of consciousness are so offensive to others that they are readily labeled psychotic so that they may more likely be put away.

All other non-psychotic counselees either care for themselves with at least minimum effectiveness or they don't offend us so much that we put them away.

In summary, the severest forms of psychopathological behavior, the psychosis, is most likely found in counselee's with neurological deficiencies, but how these people have learned to compensate for their deficiencies determines whether or not they will be labeled as psychotic.

The diagnosis is based upon the obvious ineffectiveness or the offensiveness of their behavior.

Defective neurophysiology might or might not be a significant contributing factor in the development of the other severe forms of psychopathology, psychopathy and Character Disorders. But the characterizing tendency for such individuals is their inability or unwillingness to delay gratification. They are diagnosed by their history of impulsive socially or personally ineffective or destructive behaviors. For all psychopathological counselees, whether or not medication is required to manage excessive arousal, the ultimate goal is more effective use of consciousness.

All the Rest of Us

The majority of the people who come to see psychological helpers, however, are not psychotics, psychopaths, sociopaths, or character disorders. The majority probably would not even be saddled with the less pejorative diagnosis, "neurotic." Most people who seek psychological help are often no less effective than those who do not seek psychological help. In fact, people seeking the help of psychological counselors are for the most part more intelligent, healthier, perhaps wiser, and certainly more trusting than those who do not seek such help. All of these people, however, are less effective than they need or wish to be in the use of consciousness. Therefore, as has been indicated, the primary role of the psychological helper with *all* counselees is to be creative in finding ways to enable counselees to be more effective in the use of consciousness.

What is it that enables the psychological helper to help others? The primary ingredient is, of course, the counselee's willingness to make him or herself available for such help. Therefore, the counselee must come to counseling willing to trust the psychological helper or the psychological helper must quickly engender such feelings of trust in the counselee.

Once the trust-worthiness of the psychological helper has been established in the mind of the counselee then the specific techniques used by psychological helpers are almost as numerous as the psychological helpers themselves. Although the emphasis in this theory is on improving the use of consciousness, and it would seem that some variation of cognitive therapy would be most appropriate, it should be remembered that consciousness is a synthesis of the Cerebral-Self and the Limbic-Self. Unless the psychological helper is also able to enable the counselee to manage his or her feelings, effective use of consciousness will not proceed. Indeed, the initial task of the psychological helper, the establishment of trust, is an example of the effective management of feelings. Therefore, the psychological helper must work with reasoning *and* with feelings.

You will recall that effective use of consciousness fails because anxiety or other emotions are at the time so overwhelming, or were so overwhelming in the past, that the individual short-circuits the use of consciousness in order to more quickly reduce the intensity of these emotions. Therefore, as has been said, one of the most useful tools for the psychological helper is the positive self-process—that is, mentation-for-the-sake-of-mentation, non-cerebral activation of positive limbic system states, and self-suspension. Any activity that enables the counselee to use consciousness, while at the same time managing emotions, or to suspend consciousness so that consciousness will eventually be more effective, will enable the individual to become more effective in the habitual use of consciousness. Therefore, the psychological helper is often a teacher of such techniques as meditation, recreation, or exercise.

When to End Therapy Although it may be tempting to prolong assisting these otherwise psychologically sound counselees, the sooner the effective use of consciousness can be turned over to these people, the less money they will have to spend and the more self-confidence and self-respect they will gain. With these people, the psychological helper may only need to outline appropriate cognitive strategies and guide and encourage the counselee through the beginning trials with those strategies. These counselees then become motivated by their success in the use of consciousness and no longer need psychological help.

The Abused There is, however, a group of essentially non-pathological individuals who will benefit for long-term care. These are counselees who have the capacity for effective use of consciousness but whose chronic failure to use consciousness has provided them with little opportunity to develop cognitive skills. Battered partners, abused children, and adults abused in childhood are examples of such counselees. In this group are also counselees who were abused in more subtle psychological ways by negativistic or pessimistic parents who, in an apparent attempt to encourage their children constantly criticized them, until these counselees' self-concepts have become pervasively negative. So many aspects of these counselee's lives have been associated with negative feelings about the self that the process of reinforcing positive aspects of the self, through therapy, must continue while the counselee gradually accumulates success in the use of consciousness.

This long-term, "good parent," treatment of these desperately needed people, for whom most anything the therapist gives is more than the counselee was given before, also puts the therapist at great risk of countertransference. This risk will be discussed later.

Psychotherapy for the Satisfaction of Needs

Helping at Different Levels of Integration

Wherever these essentially normal counselees are in their self-development when the begin counseling, or even when counseling with psychopathological counselees, the goal of psychological help is the eventual development of an effectively integrated self. This means that the development of such an effectively integrated self must usually begin with a physically intact Limbic-Self, capable of efficient self-arousal and the activation of both positive and negative affect. The negative affect, for example anxiety, would be capable of motivating the individual to initiate self-protective action. The positive affect would motivate the individual to continue self-integration. Then the Cerebral-Self would contain adequate information to interact effectively with the external world. The Invested-Self would become articulated clearly enough to facilitate efficient interaction with the external world and would be predominantly associated with positive affect from the Limbic-Self. The Functional-Self would be relatively unimpeded by excessive use of psychological coping mechanisms and also associated with positive limbic system affect so that the Functional-Self would be a preferred condition of the self. Likewise, the Self-Aware-Self would be a frequent process of the self, resulting in the development of clearly articulated self-concepts. The self-concepts would be sufficiently prioritized and abstracted so as to result in relatively conflict-free values. The eventual result would be an Integrated-Self capable of efficient decision-making in the complex social world. Finally, this effective self would be one that is moving toward self-transcendence so as to avoid the trap of the excessively self-contained Integrated-Self.

The purpose of this effectively integrated self is of course the maintenance and enhancement the living organization. But, more specifically, the self enables human beings to satisfy their needs. Psychopathology may also be thought of as neurophysiological impairment or behavioral ineffectiveness that interferes with the satisfaction of needs. This way of thinking about psychopathology allows a convenient way of categorizing types of psychopathology and their recommended treatments. By grouping psychopathological conditions according to the level of need-satisfaction being impeded, the complexity of skills needed to overcome the pathological impairment or behavior are also hierarchically arranged. The higher the level the need-satisfaction being impeded, the higher the level of the integration needed to undo the psychopathology.

Psychopathology Associated with the Internally Motivated Survival Needs

Psychopathologies that interfere with the satisfaction of the Internally Motivated Survival Needs are of two types: neurophysiological ineffectiveness and informational ignorance. People with impaired neurophysiology, such as the mentally retarded or brain damaged, are obviously reduced in their capacity to satisfy their basic physiological needs. Likewise, children are naturally at various levels in the development of skills for satisfying their physiological needs, although some have already developed faulty need-satisfying habits, such as enuresis or encopresis. Less obvious, however, is the ignorance or lack of information demonstrated by some people who are ineffective in maintaining their physical health because they don't eat properly, rest properly, or even breathe properly. Such people, perhaps because of ignorance but also because of the excessive use of denial, are insensitive to the cues coming from their bodies informing them of need-deprivation. Bulimia, anorexia, and colitis are types of diagnoses at this need level. The role of the psychological helper with such people is that of educator and trainer. Behavior modification is one example. Failure to learn more effective skills in satisfying these lower-order needs may lead to the cumulative physical damage that is eventually diagnosed as such psychophysiological conditions as ulcers, chronic headaches, lower back pain, and even depression. This kind of ineffective lifestyle, that consists of improper eating, elimination, breathing, and physical activity, gradually deteriorates organ systems and general health in ways that involve the whole system and makes specific diagnosis and treatment difficult to assign. In the absence of such specific physical diagnosis often such patients are referred to psychological helpers as being neurotic. Since the help needed is education or retraining rather than medication these referrals are appropriate, though the label is probably inappropriate. There might or might be any secondary gain, the indicator of psychoneurosis, associated with this ineffective behavior. But the psychodynamics underlying this psychopathology is probably less concerned with relationship to others, as is typical of psychoneurosis, than it is with relationship to the Self—as-Functional-Self that has failed to develop more effective solutions to survival needs.

Psychopathology Associated with the Externally Motivated Survival Needs

Lifestyle ignorance is also a factor in the ineffective satisfaction of the Externally Motivated Survival Needs. The threat to the satisfaction of these needs comes from outside of the body, as for example the high stress demands of a risk-filled lifestyle. Unless we were properly trained, the inclination, as we learn to satisfy our Externally Motivated Survival

Needs, is to learn techniques that provide immediate gratification, or immediate release from the anxiety associated with the threat to these needs. For example, when a bully threatens us, we learn to fight back or to run away. Such techniques offer immediate relief, but the first choice endangers us from the bully's counter aggression and the second might undermine our self-esteem. The sophisticated skill of asserting oneself, of learning to resolve conflict verbally rather than physically, requires foregoing immediate gratification. Assertiveness training is an appropriate treatment for such individuals. Likewise, the skill of pacing oneself in dealing with stressful situations requires enduring delayed gratification. So delaying gratification is an essential component of such life perpetuating lifestyle skills as proper rest, as well as proper eating and exercise.

In addition to the inappropriate use of immediate gratification to obtain physical safety, the tendency to seek immediate gratification obviously underlies the development of ineffective psychological coping mechanisms to defend against anxiety. Since using such mechanisms may undermine self-esteem, and therefore cause anxiety, and it would seem that counselees would want to give up such mechanisms. But when the self is already burdened with negative self-concepts, far more intense anxiety accompanies the terrible feeling of lost continuity of the self that is associated with losing self-control, of experiencing the disintegration of the self. For such a fragile self, learning even psychopathological coping mechanisms to *immediately* reduce anxiety would seem appropriate, and it is understandable that such counselees have difficulty in giving up such defenses. Willingness to experiment with more effective coping mechanisms would require fortunate life events that would provide counselees with long-term security while they experiment. Such fortunate events don't often occur. So the formal or informal intervention of a psychological helper is usually required.

Overcoming the counselee's resistance to change when a counselee is habituated to the use of psychopathological coping mechanisms requires considerable effort on the part of the psychological helper and dedication and courage on the part of the counselee. This of course is the classical arena psychotherapy. Overcoming resistance to change requires the most sophisticated skills of classical psychoanalysis, Rogerian therapy, and behavior modification, or the more modern cognitive behavioral techniques. The rule here is use whatever works. Whereas eclecticism in theory may be ill advised, eclecticism in treatment modality is an absolute necessity. The variety and ingenuity in the counselee's mechanisms for resisting change is such that even greater creative endeavor is needed to overcome that resistance. Such heroic effort, however, is necessary if many people are to go beyond fixation at this need level, and continue to a higher-level integration of self.

Psychopathology Associated with The Externally Satisfied Self-Enhancement Needs

In order to develop positive self-concepts, we need to be told by the world that we are okay. This external affirmation of the self may come in the form of feedback from our successful interactions with the external world, but a large portion of external affirmation comes from the positive way that others react to us. Genetics play a part in the satisfaction of this need. Those who are blessed with genetically determined physical attractiveness, intellectual quickness, or calm temperaments will probably be cherished by their parents and other adults as cute, bright, and adorable. Such people will find it easy to elicit this kind of response and thereby gain confidence in themselves, as their behavior continues to engender self-affirmation. Therefore, they may not only feel attractive but capable as well. Such confidence may further encourage such people to attempt new challenges and make it more likely that they will continue to be relatively more successful than not. As adults, these genetically fortunate people should have predominantly positive self-concepts.

Those who are not blessed with obvious physical attractiveness, intellectual quickness, or amenable temperaments may be fortunate enough to have wise parents, parents who lavish their children with affirmation even in the absence of genetic attractiveness. With such support, these less fortunate individuals may still have the courage to attempt challenges and thereby begin to accrue affirmation solely on their accomplishments.

For others, however, developing positive self-concepts is a much more painful process. Even when blessed by genetics, some people are cursed by punitive and inconsistent parents or other interpersonally destructive adults who may be struggling to offset their own negative self-concepts by taking advantage of helpless children. One common pathological parenting behavior is that of the parent whose sense of self-worth is dependent upon the child's success. As long as the child is succeeding, the parent feels good about him or herself, and excessive praise may be lavished upon the child. But let the child's success falter and the parent might become overly demanding and punitive. This oscillation between affirmation and assault might leave the child reluctant to take the risks that are necessary to continue the development of positive self-concepts.

The role of the psychological helper in assisting the person with psychopathology associated with Externally Satisfied Enhancement Needs is to a large extent that of being the "good parent." This role should be one of "conditional" positive regard. The counselee is accepted as one who is worthy of respect in that he or she is respected enough to be given information that is either positive or negative but always as accurate as the psychological helper is capable of giving. The therapeutic interaction consist largely of reevaluating feedback that has been given to the counselee in the past so that both the excesses of praise and the undeserved rejections can be checked against the opinions of one who is *not* pathologically dependent upon the counselee.

But most of the opportunities for affirmation and enhancement of the self-concepts will occur outside of the therapeutic interaction. The other role of the psychological helper with these counselees is that of a consultant in setting up interpersonal situations that have a good probability of being affirming. The task here is one of assisting the counselee in learning how to interact effectively with others, while shoring up the counselee's damaged self-confidence enough that the counselee will be able to endure those rejections that will still occur. With effective planning upon the part of the counselee and the psychotherapist, these rejections should be relatively fewer than in the counselee's past and not so overwhelming as to frighten the counselee back into his or her old self-protecting but self-defeating behaviors.

Psychopathological Relationships Counselees who have been damaged in childhood by inconsistent parents are at special risk of developing ineffective relationships as adults. Let's elaborate on this tendency. Relationship may be used in many ways to maintain and enhance the human organization. Some of these ways are ineffective. The psychopathological adult relationship is one of these ineffective attempts to satisfy the Externally Satisfied Self-Enhancement Needs. To understand how, it is necessary to clarify the general nature of relationships. On the interpersonal level, a relationship is the behavioral interaction between two or more individuals. On the intrapersonal level, however, a relationship is an extension of the self. This extension might or might not be a self-transcending extension. Most relationships function to affirm a desired concept of the existing self rather than to transcend the self. But relationships also function to satisfy lower-order needs. Infants obviously depend upon relationships with adults to satisfy survival needs. But adults also use relationships to satisfy such needs. Friends, partner, spouses, and other family members may depend upon each other to accomplish survival activities together better than they could as individuals.

Psychopathological relationships *are those that develop to manage anxiety without contributing to the continued integration of the human* *organization of one or more individuals in the relationship.* As an aspect of the self, a relationship functions as any other aspect of the self. There is a strong feeling of belongingness associated with the relationship, and that complex lambda system interrelation between the limbic system belongingness and the Cerebral Self self-concept about the relationship makes the individual sensitive to any deviation from predictions or expectations related to the relationship. When the other partner in the relationship does not act as expected, the individual is likely to become threatened. If the individual is dependent upon the other person in the relationship for satisfaction of powerful needs, anxiety is likely to be considerable.

The expectation that one should be able to depend upon the other person or persons in the relationship may be a very functional expectation. Infants, in the natural course of their development, thrive on the expectation that their parents will take care of them. Also, adult partners, spouses, or family members can often function with heightened effectiveness if they are in interdependent relationships and therefore able to depend upon others in the relationship to do for them what they cannot conveniently do for themselves. Psychopathology and its accompanying anxiety occurs in a relationship when people continue to be dependent upon someone who is not dependable or when they, in depending upon others for things that they could do for themselves, fail to develop necessary self-sufficiency.

The conflict and animosity that is typical of psychopathological relationships is a product of these inappropriate expectations. Conversely, and more constructively, when the expectations of a nonpsychopathological individual are not met, the individual comes to accept the futility of the expectations or of the relationship, and the relationship is modified and the expectation are likewise changed. In other words, the Invested-Self might no longer include the other person, and the powerful feeling of belongingness formerly associated with that aspect of the self will no longer be activated. Hence the affectively loaded expectations no longer occur. In the person with the habit of psychopathological relationships, this practical change in the Invested-Self does not readily occur. The confident self-concept does not exist that would facilitate such a change in the Invested-Self. When faced with the anxiety associated with the unmet expectation, some psychological coping mechanism is used to mitigate the anxiety. The individual may deny that the expectation was not met, rationalize away the episode, or project the source of the anxiety on to some non-self excuse. But more than likely, the psychopathological individual will attempt to manipulate or force the other person in the relationship to satisfy the expectation. Moreover, since anger is a natural physiological antagonistic state to anxiety, anger may replace the anxiety. **Anger** *is an arousal state that is naturally associated with assertive or aggressive action.* Now the demands on the other person in the relationship might be accompanied by anger and aggression. Often the other person will respond in kind, and the initial disinclination to comply with the expectation might become an adamant refusal.

These conflicts are complicated and exacerbated by the fact that all of the partners in psychopathological relationships are frequently inefficient and ineffective in satisfying their needs without the other person or persons in the relationship. Psychological helpers attempt to assist the person in a psychopathological relationship just as they attempt to alleviate any other psychopathological behavior. Anxiety is managed so that consciousness may be facilitated. The approach is often at first very directive as counselees are assisted in learning the skill and in taking the risks of doing things on their own. When anxiety is somewhat lessened, consciousness is freer to examine the unrealistic and self-defeating expectations. This in turn enables the counselees to risk even more independent behavior, subsequently resulting in further change in the self-concept. The desired end-result is a new self-concept that defines the self as competent and independent of the former psychological relationship. At this point, the decision may be made whether or not it is to the benefit of a counselee to continue in a relationship with his or her partner *or* to attempt the establishment of another relationship.

Psychopathology Associated With the Internally Satisfied Self-Enhancement Needs

The person who has avoided or overcome psychopathology associated with the Externally Satisfied Self-Enhancement Needs must only continue facing and generally overcoming the challenges that life presents, and through this process, positive self-concepts will be developed. The psychopathology that could develop at this level of self-integration is the result of too much success in affirming the self rather than too little. In our modern affluent world, where most lower-order need-fulfilling activities are handled by our technology, the person who has mastered these technologies is potentially faced with a considerable amount of meaningless time. If such a person is also no longer dependent upon others for self-affirmation, that person might find it tempting and convenient to fill that empty time with those activities that most easily affirm the self. These are activities that contribute to the reassuring sameness that is the self-contained Integrated-Self, the reassuring sameness that comes from reifying the self by always behaving consistently with one's self-concepts.

As was indicated earlier, the efficiency with which the narrowly self-contained Integrated-Self can affirm itself frees up too much time, too much time even to be filled by the self-affirming activities of the Reified I. The consequence is the anxiety of meaninglessness that might drive the individual into oblivion-seeking.

Most individuals suffering from the psychopathology of the Reified I do no seek the assistance of a psychological helper. Should this condition occur in a person of middle years, others who are dependent upon such a person or who can make use of such a person usually present that person with new challenges, new demands that will force the afflicted person into beginning the process of transcending the narrowly self-contained Integrated-Self. Young Richard Corys may, after all, only appear in ironic poems. The person afflicted with this condition who is likely to be seen by a psychological helper is one who, however, might not be recognized as having this condition. The potentially destructive occurrence of this condition is most likely in the elderly. The elderly person who has been successful in life has often gained a great portion of that success and the opportunity for self-affirmation through work. When work is terminated through retirement, there might be a sudden loss in the little self-sustaining meaningful activity still available to the individual. The primarily integrated self was already excessively self-contained in the non-work sphere. This sudden loss of meaningful activity might thrust the person into despair.

The task of the psychological helper with such counselees is that of overcoming their resistance to seeking new horizons, a resistance that might be exacerbated by the frailties of their aging bodies. The preoccupation with physical concerns is frequently the oblivion-seeking activity of choice among the elderly sufferer of this psychopathology of the excessively self-contained Integrated-Self. The challenge is one of convincing the counselees that it is worthwhile to endure the discomforts of the body and the anxiety associated with disruption in the carefully maintained self-integration so that the new meaningfulness that will inevitably come from the challenge of striving for the transcendent goal will drive out the ultimate despair of meaninglessness.

A Model Psychotherapeutic Session

An effective psychotherapeutic session must begin with the establishment of the counselee's trust in the psychotherapist. Without trust, psychotherapy is a contest rather than a cooperative partnership, a contest in which no one wins. Without trust, even psychotropic medication is likely to be ineffective since much of the medication's effects is based on the placebo effect, and the placebo effect is based on trust. So what is the most effective way to establish the counselee's trust in the psychological helper? *Give the trust that you wish to receive.* Model the trusting behavior by trusting the counselee—even before the counselee has earned that trust. After all, trust isn't necessary when you know the other person is trustworthy. Trust means risking without certainty.

But if you don't yet know if the counselee can be trusted to make wise decisions, isn't that too great a risk? Isn't the helper ethically responsible for protecting counselees from harming themselves? Yes and no. If you believe that you should protect counselees from themselves, then you are trying to do far more than is possible. You are playing God, and even God lets us make our own mistakes. No, your ethical responsibility is to honestly and openly share your concerns with counselees when counselee might be behaving irresponsibly and trust that the counselees will protect themselves. To do otherwise is to tell counselees that you do not trust them.

Next, if psychotherapy is to be effective, there must be mutual respect. The counselee must respect the psychological helper's competence and integrity, and the psychological helper must respect that the counselees are, within the limits of their current capacity, doing their best.

The psychological helper has the power to respect counselees but no power to guarantee that the counselees will be willing to respect the psychological helper. So what behavior on the part of the psychological helper is most likely to engender such respect? Here is what I believe. *Nothing is more likely to gain counselees' respect than behavior that demonstrates that the psychological helper is listening.* Moreover, I also believe that nothing is more therapeutic for counselees than knowing that someone has finally listened and heard what they have for so long been trying to say.

Value Free Psychotherapy?

Nothing in human relations is value free, and psychotherapy is no exception. Certainly the psychological helper has no right to impose values on a counselee, but even that rule is necessarily violated. The helper must structure the therapeutic session so as to enable maximum benefit to the counselee. This means imposing the helper's value of attendance and punctuality. The helper must also impose the legal and ethical values associated with psychotherapy: e.g. the helper will not support the counselee in lying, stealing, or harming others. Then there might be less obvious values psychotherapists hold that they will be tempted to impose, such as the belief that the expression of feelings is good. Undoubtedly, all psychotherapists also have other values that even they have not clearly articulated to themselves. So how does the psychological helper guard against unwarranted imposition of values onto counselees?

The strategy I use is sharing my values, the relevant ones in the beginning of the initial session and then anytime I make suggestions about how the counselee might behave to be more effective. The two initially shared values are regarding confidentiality and informed consent. I inform counselees I will not share, without their permission, whatever they reveal to me, *unless* they reveal that they intend to harm others. Regarding informed consent, I use no exotic or esoteric techniques with counselees, but I will definitely encouraging their adopting my value of effective consciousness.

The timing of sharing values is part of the art of psychotherapy. Counselees are usually eager to start telling their stories, and might not even register your discussion on the above psychotherapeutic values. Suspicious or insecure counselees might need to be told right away about confidentiality and informed consent. Just be alert to cues from the counselee.

Values of Effective Consciousness

The goal of psychotherapy is enabling the counselee to becoming effectively conscious so as to overcome dysfunctional actions and feelings. As has been frequently stated, numerous counseling skills must be used by the helper to enable the counselee to progress toward this goal. Although it has also been stated that the helper should not impose values on counselees, these are the values that I nevertheless offer my counselees and hope that they will adopt.

1. If a person is to be effectively conscious that person must seek awareness and mastery of his or her thoughts and feelings so that both thoughts *and* feelings are available in making decisions to enable surviving and thriving.
2. A person has the right to feel whatever he wishes and is capable of feeling.
3. But experiencing a feeling does not require that the person act upon that feeling.
4. As such, a person is free to choose whatever he wishes or is capable of feeling.

5. *Responding* to a feeling is usually preferable to reacting to a feeling, since reacting gives the person little time to effectively manage the feeling through the use of thought. Responding means consciously considering the consequence of one's response before acting.

6. Failure to allow oneself to be aware of one's feelings deprives one of information needed to make effective decisions, e.g. to be effectively conscious.

7. Since people are capable of being effectively conscious, that is, capable of being aware of both thoughts and feelings, if they have not been rendered unconscious by someone or ineffectively conscious by something beyond their control, (i.e. psychosis, dementia, or cerebra trauma) then people should be held responsible for any actions that are prompted by either their thoughts or feelings.

8. In other words, people who have intoxicated themselves, or who have allowed themselves to react to their feelings without thinking, or who have denied their feelings are still responsible for their dysfunctional feelings and the actions that are be motivated by those feelings.

You will notice that, assuming the primacy of feelings, effective consciousness is primarily effective management of feelings. But those whose inclination and strength is cognition needn't despair. Most of the tools in the psychotherapeutic process are cognitive. These cognitive tools are necessary means to the end of positive feelings.

The Psychotherapeutic Steps

Keeping these effective consciousness values in mind, typically here's what I do in a psychotherapeutic session:

After welcoming the counselee, and explaining confidentiality and informed consent as warranted, I usually ask, "How can I help?"

Most of the time, counselees are eager to tell their story, and I listen until the counselee winds down. If the counselee is reluctant to self-disclose or ceases talking with little said, I become more directive. I ask in what way the counselee is in pain, and if necessary suggest words that might describe the pain. Almost never is anything else needed to begin the story and continue it until the counselee apparently feels that enough have been told. Then counselees usually pull out of themselves, look at the psychological helper and expect answers; they expect to be told what to do. After all, that's why they came to the expert.

What I do then, I believe, takes even more expertise than being the authority who gives expert advise. I demonstrate that I have truly been listening. As succinctly but as comprehensively as possible, I summarize everything the counselee has said. I begin with a statement that admits I may not have heard everything and also implies that I want to be sure that I'm not too far off in my interpretation. I say something like, "Let me tell you what I think I've heard you say."

I believe that my psychotherapeutic summary is one of the most effective tools I have as a therapist. Moreover, eschewing false modesty, I believe I am very effective in summarizing, since I've been practicing this skill for more than thirty years. But my effectiveness is only possible because I really do listen.

A Sample Summary

Here's a typical psychotherapeutic summary, with a twenty-five year old male who is just getting started in a career. He is rather homely, and he has been rejected by his girlfriend of four months, the first significant relationship he has ever had. He is obviously dejected, not sleeping well, has no appetite, and is skipping meals. He has also neglected his appearance, and is no longer exercising. His boss has called him in several times regarding his tardiness and lessening production. He fears that he is in danger of being fired. He wasn't enthusiastic about seeking help, but his mother is disgusted and angry at his behavior, and she insisted.

After he has told his story, during which time my eyes would have seldom left him, here's what I might say: "Bill, let me tell you what I think I've heard you say. You've always been cautious about getting involved with a woman, mostly because you didn't believe you had much of a chance. Growing up, a few girls even made fun of your looks. Now, for the first time, you thought you'd found a girl who wasn't hung up on looks, so you took a chance and let yourself start caring. Now, she told you she's changed her mind, and no matter what you've said, her mind's made up. She just wants to be friends.

"Now you know why you'd always been reluctant to get involved. You suspected that rejection would hurt—but not this much. First you were shocked, then angry. You didn't tell her how angry you were, but you were certainly very cold when you hung up the phone. The anger didn't last very long, however. Then the hurt took over; you even started crying. When you pulled yourself together, you called her back. She just repeated what she had said, so you hung up again, and vowed to never call her again.

"It didn't take you long to get desperate, however. Now you've called so many times she's even saying that you're harassing her, and she's hinting that she might file a complaint.

"Since that time, things have gone down hill. Your mother's disgusted with you, your boss is annoyed with you, and you're not too happy with yourself, either. Most of all, you feel rotten helpless, hopeless, and weak. You even ache all over, like maybe you're coming down with something.

"Is that most of what you've told me?"

Bill, who has been listening intently, nods yes.

I continue. "It sounds rather unpleasant, but also all very normal. No body enjoys being rejected, and even the most self-confident person experiences at least some degree of what you've described. But, you've also honestly told me you're not all that self-confident. You think you're homely, and you fear that somehow you've blown your first and last chance at a worthwhile relationship. But let's see how real that is. Yes, from what you've told me, this first risk at a relationship appears to be over. Getting her back doesn't seem very promising, at least not anytime soon. So what else might you be working on? Let me suggest that, for the time being, the first objective is to stop hurting. Then, after the pain is no longer sapping your energy, the next objective might be getting you back into a position to have options other than just wallowing in your misery, maybe even moving on to another relationship."

Bill shakes his head, and seems about to object. He apparently isn't ready to consider another relationship.

Before he voices is lack of confidence, I continue. "Before you decide on your next step, let' see what you've got going for you. You've told me you used to be in good physical condition. You know how to take care of yourself. Although you're feeling rotten now, I don't believe you've damaged yourself yet. Check with your physician if you have doubts. Next, although you don't much care for yourself right now, there are people who do care. Your mother cares enough to be angry at you. Your boss cared enough to be up front and to semi-threat firing you. It appears he still expects you to do better, which seems to suggest that he would rather keep than fire you. Even your ex-girlfriend cared enough to be honest with you. Then she put up with your *persistence* perhaps longer than she should have. So, you must not be a totally unacceptable person. Right?"

He smiles.

"Finally, as I've already said, what you're experiencing is hardly usually, and your response isn't either. Even though you're seeing a Psychologist, you're not abnormal. In fact, since you've agreed to seek help you've demonstrated, in my admittedly biased opinion, a good deal of courage and wisdom."

Bill even manages a chuckle this time.

"So let's get started. You've gotten past your first major hurdle; you come to see me. But, frankly, you still look all tensed up and in pain. Let me show you something. Why don't you just take a deep breath, and sit back an relax as you slowly let out the breath."

He doesn't yet move.

"No, I mean it. Just breathe deeply, and relax. Do it!"

He complies.

Now, keep breathing…relax…breathe relax…."

"Good. Now be aware of how you feel, and tell me."

"Better. But so what? I also feel better when I finally fall asleep, but then I have to wake up, and it starts all over again."

"Perhaps true, but what I wanted you to know is that you *can* change the way you feel, however temporarily. So, since you said you want to stop hurting, let's see if we can find a way to extend the time you feel better. Simply breathing makes your feel better. What else makes you feel better?

"I don't know."

"Yes you do. Breathing for a longer time makes you feel better. You feel better after you exercise, right? You feel better after you eat, a least a small meal, right?"

"Right."

"Then here's what I want you do. Right now, describe a plan and schedule for how you are going to eat, exercise, and stop to breathe regularly so as to break up the tension you have been holding on to. While you are at it, also include in your schedule getting up early to get work, thanking your boss for fussing at you, and even thanking your mother for being disgusted with you."

He laughs. "Well, okay, but I still don't have a girlfriend."

"True, but you will be on your way to being someone a girlfriend would want as a boyfriend.

"So, doesn't this all make sense?"

Yeah, I guess."

"No, I believe you *know* it makes sense. I suspect that nothing I've said to you surprises you. I've just told back to you what you told me, though obviously stated in a positive way rather than the gloom and doom story you gave me. Now, let's do this. If you'd like, make another appointment, and come back and tell me exactly what you did, and how you felt. Remember, no matter what happens, you can't lose. You'll learn what worked or even what didn't work, so you won't waste time doing that again."

The Psychotherapeutic Summary

The psychotherapeutic summary has four parts: a description of the pain, a statement of the counselee's objectives, the encapsulation of the current problem, and a positive reframing of the therapeutic challenge.

The Pain Most counselees come to counseling knowing that they want to reduce their pain, but the pain may be too broadly felt, having spread to too many aspects of their lives for them to describe it succinctly or accurately. My task, in the summary, is to very specifically describe the most intense and *current* pain, a pain that can be alleviated in a reasonable amount of time. Pain is hard to describe. Often counselees lack the vocabulary to label what they are feeling. Words like fear, helplessness, anxiety, or depression mean different things to different people. Without words to describe their pain, counselees lack power to understand and manage their pain. Poets call upon metaphors to help others experience the poet's unique pain. So the psychological helper must be an expert in the language of feelings, particularly the feeling of pain, and perhaps even a minor poet. The purpose of this art, however, is not to entertain or even to inspire, but is always to insure the counselees that you have truly been listening. As proof of how well you have been listening, you now accurately express your counselees' unique pain in words, words that can give them power over their pain.

The Objective Most counselees have been struggling to understand why they are in pain, and most have also taken the logical steps that proceed from their understanding, trying to do what their understanding of the problem indicates they should do to solve the problem causing the pain—and nothing has worked. In fact, most of the time, before they are driven to risk counseling, *many* such counselee-developed therapeutic theories and plans have failed miserably, and now the counselees are desperate—something has to change. But what is this change? Effective use of consciousness in psychotherapy cannot begin until what is intended to be accomplished is clearly understood, and of course that goal will not be reached unless it is reachable. Pain reduction is obviously the goal of psychotherapy, but this is a byproduct of the actions taken by the counselee. The counselees need to know how to act or, in other words, they need to have doable objectives. My task in the psychotherapeutic summary is to state such doable objectives.

The Current Problem But too often the counselees' theories and plans are based on distorted or unrealistic reasoning. They have looked for causes outside of themselves, over which they have no control, so naturally in their powerlessness they fail. My task is to summarize the history of the problem given by the counselees, so as to show respect for the counselee's heroic efforts, but to focus on and encapsulate those aspects of the problem over which they *do* have control.

The Positive Reframing Counselees usually come to counseling with at an overwhelming awareness of their pain, but they also have as least a vague understanding of what is causing their pain and some idea of what they should do reduce the pain. But since even with this much awareness nothing has worked they have begun to lose hope. The positive reframing of the problem restores hope. Of course, for psychological helpers to reframe positively, they must themselves be positive, they must themselves believe that the counselee has the ability to solve the problem, if given support, encouragement, and the necessary cognitive tools. From that positive core, while listening to the counselee's story, the helper is continually focused on the counselees' strengths rather than weaknesses, on anything that can be done rather than on what can't or shouldn't be done.

It is undoubtedly obviously from this description of a psychotherapeutic summary that I won't be offering a step-by-step process for developing an effective summary. Effectively summarizing all that the counselee has just said is an art and not a science. It is like a musical composition and not the result of applying an engineering formula. Like improvisation on a violin, it takes years of practice. So how do you know you have created a work of art when you have given a psychotherapeutic summary?

Your audience, *the counselee tells you.*

Knowing Success

For the psychological helper, this is the moment of truth, and perhaps the moment of greatest reward. If you have truly listened and summarized what you have heard, the counselee might first looks surprised, even startled. *This person was really listening! Finally!* Then, insofar as this damaged person is still able to show feelings, the expression on the counselee's face says "Thank you!"

But of course, proud and happy as I may be, I don't leave it at that. Although I am struggling to be a therapeutic artist, I am also a trained social scientist. I must try to validate my assumptions. I might ask, "Is that what you told me, and does the way I said it back to you make sense?"

Most of the time my counselees make few modifications of what I have said. Usually, even with their modifications, counselees are ready for my next question. "Well, if that accurately describes the problem, what should *you* do about it?"

Most counselees then come up with a logical action plan. The positive reframing usually suggests such a plan. Sometimes it is something not tried before, sometimes it is a previously failed plan, but one that will now be more narrowly focused and supported by a positive attitude, with renewed hope.

Obviously, the mere statement of a plan is still not enough. There must be commitment and above all there must be action. I usually say, "Tell me again *exactly* what you plan to do. I want to hear details of when and how you plan to act."

At this point, the teacher may take over. I will use role-playing, having counselees practice what they will say or do, and I will respond as the significant other in the problem (more artistic work) or as an objective observer.

After training the counselee, I try to foster commitment and the consequent action by suggesting: "Let's do this. If you'd like, come back next week at tell me what you did. I expect you will tell me, 'Hey it worked. I'm on my way. I don't need you anymore.' Or you will tell me, 'It didn't work—it was the dumbest thing I ever did.' Either way, you didn't lose. If what you tried failed, you learned what doesn't work. So then we'll come up with a new plan."

Direct Management of Feelings

The effective use consciousness is obviously concerned with the effective management of feelings to enable the counselee to survive and eventually feel fulfillment in life. But hindering the successful management of feelings are misconceptions about feelings, the most debilitating of which is the belief that one is *compelled* to feel. This is indicated in the common statement, "I can't help the way I feel." It is true that some feelings are reflexive or overlearned, and the feelings occur before consciousness can intervene. But we are not compelled to continue experiencing feelings that might have been *triggered* by events or people beyond our control. When a reckless driver cuts in front of you, you will likely feel fear, then anger or even outrage. But you might then *choose* to feel disgusted or even amused at the foolishness of some people.

Effective use of consciousness would suggest that you choose to feel whatever will enable you to act wisely, to slow down and avoid that driver rather than roaring into road rage and ramming the reckless rogue. (Sorry about that alliteration. The Therapeutic-Poet made me do it.)

But under the influence of powerful feelings such as fear or anger, or depression or jealousy, many counselees have been the victims rather than the masters of their feelings. They have seldom or never experienced success in *choosing* to feel rather than being compelled to feel. The psychological helping's task is to provide them with such success. Here is where direct management of feelings is vital and may be one of the counselee's most moving and facilitating experiences in counseling. Here's an example of such an intervention with the depressed counselee. The thoughts that accompany depression have usually locked the counselee in helplessness. "What's the use; there's nothing I can do; and life's not worth living anyway." But depression is more than a state of the mind, more than just morbid thoughts. Depression is a state of the body. Baring a sudden brilliant insight, morbid thoughts and other such dysfunctional thoughts take time to alter, but a state of the body can be changed almost immediately. Here's what I do. Sometimes all that is needed is to ask the depressed counselee to breathe deeply and listen only to my voice repeating "Breathe and relax." In a short time, in spite of the counselee's habit of dwelling upon the pain, the action of breathing and relaxing various parts of the body effect a change in the body—and the pain is replaced by another feeling, the feeling of relaxation. Since relaxation is a different state of the body, one that is physiologically incompatible with depression, the counselee is *at that moment* no longer depressed. I then have the counselee focus on that surprising new feeling and point out that it was brought about simple by doing what was totally within the counselee's power to do—breathe and relax.

Of course, the feeling of depression will return. It is an overlearned or perhaps a hormonally triggered state of the body. But now the counselee knows that a different state of the body is possible. An action plan that includes meditation and exercise, both of which promote immediate change in the body's state, from pain to relief, should now seem more worthwhile to the counselee. Then, when such an action plan becomes a lifestyle, the counselee is no longer a depressed counselee, and then no longer a counselee.

These are some of the other states of the body that can be taught and immediately experienced by a counselee: exercise can bring about physical strength, endorphin-induced euphoria, and even exhaustion, all of which are physiologically incompatible with the physiological state of depression. Even anger is incompatible with depression. Meditation can produce an hypnogogic state that is the same as the initial and ending stage of sleep and is just as beneficial to the usually sleep-ineffective depressed counselee. A healthy balanced meal can also induce such an hypnogogic state.

All of these strategies for directly managing feelings are applicable to other dysfunctional feelings, such as jealousy, hatred, envy, and pessimism. Of course, medicine also changes feelings, though more slowly. Unlike medication, however, these direct feeling-management techniques have no bad side effects.

Diagnosis and the Psychotherapeutic Summary

It may be obviously by now that the psychotherapeutic summary is in fact a psychological diagnosis, but it is I believe a more useful form of diagnosis than is conventional. It is not merely a convenient shorthand for communicating with colleagues, nor is it an agreed upon label to be certain that insurance companies will pay for services. It is a working hypothesis that outlines the behavioral and psycho dynamics of the counselee so as to suggest a preliminary plan of action. Even more important, unlike the conventional diagnosis that is shared sometimes exclusively with colleagues or insurance companies, it is shared first and sometimes exclusively with the counselee. As stated, the profound effect of the psychotherapeutic summary is that it can convince counselees that they are trusted and respected.

Transference and Countertransference

When counselees have been given hope, and even before they have begun to succeed, this renewed hope is like a powerful drug. If what you have done in so short a time has changed they way they feel, made them feel better than they have felt in ages, they want more, and they want to believe that you can give it to them. And, to a degree, they are correct. You do have expertise and skill. You *can* help. In fact, since they might now be ready and eager to listen and to try the strategies you suggest, strategies they didn't have to courage or knowledge to attempt before, they will likely have even more success. Then you can use their faith in you to recommend and teach even more ambitious strategies. This intense belief in you is of course transference. Counselees begin transferring onto you the childlike faith they might have had in their parents (if they were fortunate). They give you enormous power to motivate and direct them toward their goals. So use this power—but only temporarily. Remember, the goal of the good parent is enabling the child to become independent of the parent, not to continue the dependence for the glory of the parent. Therein lies the danger of being given and using transference power in the therapeutic process. You might use it for your gains and not the counselees'.

The gain of course could be monetary, continuing the counselees' dependence to continue your income. But a more subtle misuse of power in the therapeutic process, and one that is even more destructive, is reveling in the countertransference. I am defining **countertransference** as *the mistaken belief that you are actually what the counselee wants* *to believe you are.* You *are not* the perfect parent that the counselee never had. However glorious it might feel, you are not all knowing and all wise. (And certainly you are not as desirable as some affection starved counselees want to believe.) So even while you are using the transference for the good of the counselee, you must constantly remind yourself that you are just your old fallible and non-sexy you. Do this by continuing to express your suggestions as experiments to be proven empirically and not as dogma to be followed religiously. Just as important, elicit more and more of the strategies from the counselee rather than enjoying how clever you are by creating new therapeutic strategies. Always remember, even you are subject to the seduction of countertransference, because just like your counselees you have an enormous capacity for self-deception. You too are human.

Can Counseling be Taught?

Since counseling, as described here, is an art and not a science in which formulas can be applied successfully, can anyone be taught to help others who are in profound pain to use heightened consciousness to solve their problems? Again, the answer is yes and no. I do believe the potential psychological helper must come to the process already blessed with adequate intelligence. But these additional attributes are also vital for counseling effectiveness: awareness of ones own feelings and a willingness to acknowledge even negative feelings; sensitivity to the feelings of others; skill in expressing feelings verbally and non verbally; respect, faith, and trust in others even in profoundly damaged others; and enough self-confidence and courage to risk being wrong and still willing to keep trying. Can a potential psychological helper really be taught to be and perform these ways?

If I am not to be hypocritical, the answer has to be yes. After all, isn't the acquisition of these attributes just what I have been expecting of my counselees? So shouldn't I believe that a somewhat less damaged person such as a psychological helper is also capable of learning? So the answer is yes. Moreover, even at my age, I'm also capable of continuing to learn. Therefore, what I and any other psychological helpers must do, whether in training or with years of experience, is continually remind ourselves to practice what we preach.

The Psychological Helper in a Sick Society

People, regardless of their ages, who are most subject to the psychopathology of the excessively self-containment Integrated-Self are the people most needed in a crisis that is coming.

To explain, let me give a brief review. The self evolved as a more effective tool for maintenance and enhancement of the living organization. But the self, though marvelously effective, can subvert itself to avoid anxiety and it can trap itself in immature or ineffective organizations, such as the psychopathologies. Assisting individuals to mature and to avoid and overcome psychopathology is the usual challenge of the psychological helper. The immature self and the psychopathological self seek immediate gratification and, by definition, behave irresponsibly. With proper parenting and societal support or with psychological help individuals are enabled to mature and overcome this built-in immediate gratification-seeking liability of the self. Consequently, most individuals mature and behave responsibly.

But the distinction between responsible and irresponsible behavior becomes less clear when individuals are functioning at the level of the Integrated-Self. Excessively self-contained Integrated-Selves have highly Functional-Selves. Most of their problems are handled efficiently, and the living organization of such individuals can generally be maintained until genetically determined biological limits are reached, and the so-called natural death occurs. Moreover, those who suffer from the excessively self-contained Integrated-Self, with its accompanying meaninglessness and anxiety, are likely to reach this stage when the biological time clock is already winding down, and the continued evolution of the self is not worth the pain it will cause. Therefore, it would seem that the self, even with its built-in irresponsible tendency toward excessive self-containment, has already done the job it evolved to do, and the person can die having lived a fulfilled and productive life. But there is another threat created by the self in concert with other selves that might soon undermined the success that has been made possible by the evolution of the self. Human beings, with their highly effective Functional-Selves, cooperating with other selves, have created a technology that threatens to destroy the external world from which the self evolved and which must continue to exist if other selves are to continue existing.

Nuclear technology has the potential to destroy the world almost instantaneously, and it and other forms of environmentally polluting technology threaten to do the same over an only slightly longer time period. These technologies were developed to maintain and enhance the self. But once these powerful technologies exist anyone can use them, for any purpose. Technologies that might have been developed by responsible individuals for responsible purposes are now available for use by irresponsible individuals— irresponsible or psychopathological selves who are dedicated to the pursuit of immediate gratification, of immediate reduction of anxiety or the oblivion of compulsive pleasure-seeking. In the past, such behavior, by the powerless young, was expected and usual did little damage, even to those so behaving. But modern technology may put enormous world-destroying power in the hands of adults (and adolescents) still functioning at the level of the survival needs who have not yet developed the habit of the delayed gratification that is necessary for managing such power. Such individual may seek to use these technologies to insure individual survival or immediate gratification for brief durations and in the process bring about irrevocable damage to the environment. In other words, psychopathological political leaders, in attempting to insure their physical survival or even the survival of their narrowly self-contained political self-concepts, may risk the destruction of the world by nuclear adventurism—"Better dead than red." Or industrial leaders, in attempting to insure the immediate gratification made possible by their affluent life styles or in attempting to be consistent with their corporate self-concepts, may introduce enticing technological advancements that overtax or perilously pollute the environment and hasten environmental deterioration—"What is good for General Motors is good for America." Or computer sophisticated adolescents, in attempting to gain immediate gratification of their external self-enhancement needs, may sabotage the Internet and all the environmental protection dependent upon the Internet—"SuperNerd Srikes Again."

This of course is the terrible dilemma of our times. The supreme product of the evolution of life on Earth, the human self, has evolved to the level of integration that enables life to destroy the Earth that made life possible. The highly integrated organization that is the human self might turn out to be a defective self-terminating branch of evolution. Because the human self exists, human life and perhaps even all life on Earth might cease to exist. The sovereign drive of life to maintain and enhance its organization may turn out to be thwarted by the particular pathway that human evolution has taken. Astronomers have speculated that intellectual beings whose environments make possible technological evolution will inevitably reach the point at which the destructive potential of the exponential growth of technology threatens to outpace the slower moral evolution of intelligent beings that would enable them to control the irresponsible use of technology. Therefore, if there are other intelligent beings in the universe, few or none of them might solve this problem. Intellectualism, or in other words, the use of consciousness to solve problems through logic, might be the inevitable consequence of the evolving integration of the living organization. Likewise, self-destructive technologies might also be an inevitable consequence of the evolution of living organism. Therefore life, the anomaly in the universe, that violates the law of entropy, might be in fact merely a temporary disturbance in the natural disintegration of matter that will eventually lead to universal chaos.

But frankly, *this* little speck of life in the universe is not ready to capitulate to entropy. After all, the answer is simple. All we have to do is behave responsibly. All we have to do is forego immediate gratification, use consciousness more effectively, avoid and overcome psychopathology, develop beyond the narrowly self-contained Integrated-Self, and achieve self-transcendence. Then all we have to do is enable enough of us to go beyond our individual selves to create the integrated Transcendent-Self. This is all we have to do. Nothing to it, right?

This is, of course, one of those unobtainable-within-a-lifetime transcendent goals if there ever was one. Nevertheless, the alternative consequence to failure to choose this transcendent goal makes the undertaking of such a goal a necessity.

What then is the role of the psychological helper when confronted with this sick human society? The role is that which it has always been. As with individual counselees, so with society. The psychological helper must be creative and patiently persistent in the struggle to improve the effective use of consciousness. As with the individual, so with society. Psychopathological counselees and psychopathological societies have developed self-destructive mechanisms for achieving immediate gratification rather than confronting problems. The role of the psychological helper with our society is to enable our society to forego immediate gratification in favor of delayed gratification. The role of the psychological helper with our society is to enable our society to develop strategies for enduring the anxiety accompanying the abandonment of psychopathological mechanisms, particularly the use of denial, long enough to develop more effective uses of consciousness.

This of course means that psychological helpers must themselves give up the comfortable security of their self-contained integrated professional selves and be willing to suffer the anxiety of disintegration that will be an inevitable part of identifying with so complex and remote a goal as curing our psychopathological society. Assuming that we have such courage, what strategies are likely to be effective? It is difficult enough to enable individuals to control their anxiety so that they may then develop feasible strategies for solving the problems that have caused their anxiety, but how does the psychological helper interact constructively with the myriad ineffective selves that are components of our psychopathological society? That, of course, is the creative challenge. Political advocacy is a possible choice. Seeking positions of leadership in society is another. We may also apply our existing expertise to articulate societal problems in ways that are amenable to exploration through research so that strategies to be used to assist society do not have to be tried in an untested form. Theoretical exploration, as in this book, may also contribute.

Whatever the strategies to be used, psychological helpers, with their investment in effective living and their talents, skills, and desire to assist their fellow human beings to experience and make use of their feelings and of their capacities for consciousness have a contribution to make in this struggle to maintain and enhance human life on Earth. The psychological helper is uniquely equipped to be an advocate of this creative synthesis of feelings and knowledge that must become the new social consciousness.

As I said in beginning this book, the self and that aspect of self that is consciousness could not have evolved had not life first evolved. Now it seems probable that life on Earth cannot continue to evolve unless consciousness is used to guide and impel life beyond the narrow confines of individual selves. What is beyond the self is yet to be known. What is beyond *failure to evolve beyond the self* is something that we might not wish to know.

Afterword

I wrote the first draft of this book in 1982, and then put it aside. When I partially retired I had time to revisit the person I was those many years ago. I was surprised that back then I almost had a clear grasp of what I was doing. In this updated vision, I've tried to express my ideas more clearly, and I've added what I've learned over the intervening years about clinical practice. But the core of the theory is unchanged from the original draft.

So I've done what I set out to do. I've explained to myself how and why the existence of life has led to the development of the human self and how the possibly unique expression of human life, consciousness, must be used effectively if the human self can continue to exist and perhaps transcend itself. I have also outlined how I have applied this theory as a psychotherapist, and I am satisfied that in so doing I have appropriately assisted my counselees.

Through this self-analysis I have also come to believe that there can be no step-by-step formula for a therapist to follow, and any psychotherapeutic theory that prescribes such a formula is misleading. I believe that a psychotherapist will only be successful if the way he works is an expression of his uniqueness. Therefore, this *very generally* application of a theory may well be totally unique to me, and it worked for me only because I work best in striving toward effective use of consciousness. But if you are more or less like me, if I am not so unique after all, then perhaps this book will help clarify your own thinking about what you are doing as a psychotherapist.

References

Descartes, Rene, "The History of Epistemology: Modern Philosophy,' and "The Soul, Mind, and Body: The Mind-Body Relationship," *Encyclopaedia Britanica, 1998.*

MacLean, Paul D. "Sensory and Perceptive Factors in Emotional Functions of the triune Brain," *Emotions: Their Parameters and Measurement.* New York: Raven Press, 1974.

Maslow, Abraham H. *Motivation and Personality.* New York: Harper and Row, 1954.

Sagan, Carl. *The Dragons of Eden: Speculation on the Evolution of Human Intelligence.* New York: Random House, 1977.

Sommerhoff, Gerd. *Logic of the living Brain.* London, New York: Wiley, 1974.

Index